All My Loving

All My Loving

Coming of Age
with Paul McCartney
in Paris

Beth
Kaplan

**BPS
books**

TORONTO & NEW YORK

Published in 2014 by
BPS Books
Toronto and New York
www.bpsbooks.com
A division of Bastian Publishing Services Ltd.

ISBN 978-1-927483-81-7 (paperback)
ISBN 978-1-927483-83-1 (ePUB)
ISBN 978-1-927483-82-4 (ePDF)

Cataloguing-in-Publication Data available from Library and Archives Canada.

Cover: Alanna Cavanagh
Text design and typesetting: Tannice Goddard, Soul Oasis Networking

For Eli

NOTE TO THE READER

This memoir is as true as I can make it, which is pretty true because of the voluminous paper trail that follows me wherever I go — a lifetime's trove of diaries, poems, stories, drawings and letters, saved by my pack rat mother and my pack rat self.

And so, the diary and story excerpts from 1964 and 1965, included here in italics, are quoted verbatim — except for a few instances where, in the interests of good storytelling, time has been telescoped or dates switched, and stories and diary entries pruned. A number of names have been changed and an occasional word or line modified for clarity. The spelling mistakes made then have been retained.

These are my own memories. Others who were there, especially my brother, undoubtedly remember things differently.

FROM THE SCRAPBOOK OF MY WRITINGS

December 1963, age thirteen

QUESTIONS

Will I ever
Grow up, as they say?
Will the boys
Look at me, one day?
Will my opinion
Be listened to?
Will they still say
"How you grew!"
Will my thoughts
Become less wild?
Oh, when will I
Not be a child?

1964

1

January

We were eating meatloaf — at least, they were eating and I was pretending to — when Dad shifted the mush in his mouth and turned to me. "Your mother and I have a Ban the Bomb meeting tonight, Pupik," he said. "I think the snow tires will get us there."

The most thrilling news! My parents would be going out to save the world from nuclear fallout, and the house, for a few precious hours, would be mine. Except for my little brother, who'd be playing in the snow somewhere and who didn't matter anyway.

As soon as our Morris Minor sputtered out of the driveway, I rushed back to the kitchen, switched on the radio — the news, "President Johnson blah blah blah" — and twiddled the knob until the speaker sang out "CHNS — 960 on the AM dial." The cool evening DJ Frank Cameron was announcing a song called "Little Doos Coop." How odd, I thought, guys singing high, like girls. I didn't know what a doos coop was, but for sure we didn't have any in Halifax, Nova Scotia.

I bent way over the red arborite counter, twiddling bits of hair and biting my fingernails, comforting habits that were forbidden when Dad was around, and thought about my school friend Lea

3

with her new very long bangs who always knew what was the next sharp thing. Was that a skill you just had, like being good at arithmetic? If not, how could I get it too? Lea didn't care what other people thought. She was *with* it. I envied that.

My parents fought a lot, but when Mozart came on the CBC, they got soft and quiet. My parents would really hate "Little Doos Coop."

THE DAY BEFORE, as I'd walked into Home Economics class, my mind had changed. Just like that. Listening to Lea cry, "They love jelly babies? What're jelly babies and where can I get some?" a thought flew at me and hit hard.

"You," said a voice inside, "should listen to that group too."

This time, I said yes. It was Monday, January 13, 1964, I was thirteen years, five months and thirteen days old, and yes, I would listen to that group and find out what my friends were going on about.

But how? Unlike my classmates, I didn't own a transistor radio. The only radio at my house, the square brown Philips on the kitchen counter, was guarded by my parents, always tuned to the CBC with its tweety violins and flutes. How would I get to hear the Hit Parade?

Since December, most of the girls in my class had spent every spare moment oohing and aahing over photographs of four boys with hair covering their foreheads, and swooning over the new group's songs on the Hit Parade. "Love me do," I overheard. "Please please me." "Ask me why." A bunch of strange orders.

A year younger than my classmates, I had no interest in the Hit Parade. The songs were silly. I mean, "Itsy Bitsy Teenie Weenie Yellow Polka Dot Bikini..."

"Duke duke duke duke of earl duke duke duke of earl duke duke duke of earl ..."

I mean.

When I was twelve, my best friend Vicky, who was thirteen, had begun to spend her allowance on 45s instead of on china horse figurines from Woolworth's, which we used to buy together. One day she insisted on playing me her new single, "Please Don't Talk to the Lifeguard."

"That's the stupidest song I've ever heard," I said.

"Jeepers, you're young," she said, which hurt.

What had happened to her? Why was she snapping her fingers to 45s when we, beautiful orphan sisters, should be leaping onto our horses, hers an appaloosa named Wildfire and mine a palomino named Champ, and galloping bareback around our very own island?

THAT MONDAY NIGHT, snow pelted the bedroom windows as I lay, blankets drawn tight around my neck just the way I liked, reading *The Mystery at the Moss-Covered Mansion*. Nancy Drew and I, solving mysteries with our friends Bess and George, waiting for our beau Ned Nickerson in his jaunty roadster, and making our lawyer father, dignified Mr. Drew, proud. I read late, clicked off my light and tried to sleep. When we moved into this house seven years ago, after our stay in England, my mother had chosen Twenty Wildflowers wallpaper for my little room. During many sleepless nights — I was not a sleeping kind of person — I'd memorized the pattern of those delicate pink and white flowers, repeated in their ribbony green rectangles round my bed. I traced the flowers as I tossed and turned, listening to the storm outside the house. And the one inside too. My parents, downstairs.

Through that bitter night, there was such a giant snowfall that next morning, oh heaven, school was cancelled. Tuesday, January 14, was a blessed day. After a brief attempt to clean my room, I put on my snow pants and ploughed through waist-high snow to make a snow fort and angels with Carol and her little sister Joanie, the girls next door.

After lunch, I squirrelled myself into a corner of Dad's living room armchair and re-read one of my favourite books, *Little Women*. If only I could be Beth, my namesake, dying beautifully, loved by all.

"Beth! Come set the table!" How many times that voice had blasted into my reveries, just at a good bit in a book. Supper was awful, as suppers at our house always were — tonight, meatloaf full of mysterious lumps that I suspected included onions, me swishing little bites through my mouth with lots of milk, my parents nagging about cleaning my plate, piano practice, homework.

And then, they'd gone out to ban the bomb.

FRANK CAMERON ANNOUNCED the drippy singing nun with her guitar. I liked some pop singers, I wasn't a complete lost cause. In grade five, Scott, the boy I had a crush on, got me to listen to "Teen Angel." What a tragic song, that poor girl squashed in the train wreck holding her boyfriend's ring. I liked "Venus in Blue Jeans," though no one I knew actually owned any blue jeans. Ricky Nelson with his forest of eyelashes and "Hello Mary Lou, Goodbye Heart." The Everly Brothers with my theme song — "Dre-e-e-e-eam, dreeeeam dream dream…"

"Bobby's Girl" and "Johnny Get Ang-er-y," "Big Girls Don't Cry" and "Rhythm of the Rain." Bobby Curtola. Neil Sedaka. Dion.

But I could only hear the music at my friends' houses, and anyway, who cared about bop she bop rama dinga ding ding when there were sexy Barbie paper dolls to dress up and take out dancing?

What I did after school, when homework and piano practice were done, was read, write stories and poems and in my diary, invent lives for my paper dolls and cut out and stick pictures in my stack of scrapbooks. There was a kittens and horses scrapbook, one for ballet, one for Hayley Mills — I'd seen *The Parent Trap* three times. There was a *Scrapbook of My Writings*, into which I copied out my best work.

A month ago, in December, I'd begun a serious new scrapbook, dedicated to President John Fitzgerald Kennedy. Handsome President Kennedy was the most important man in the world; beside him, our Canadian Prime Minister, Lester B. Pearson, looked like a woodchuck. On Friday, November 22, 1963, I'd left school to go home and got on the bus, to find all the passengers sobbing and holding each other. In a minute, I was sobbing too.

That great man's death was the worst thing that had ever happened in the world. In my world, anyway.

"AND NOW KIDS," said Frank, "what you've all been waiting for — the Fab Four from Liverpool! Here are the Beatles with 'She Loves You.'"

Heart whumping, I leaned in further and turned up the sound a bit. A wild rumble of drums. Voices — full of energy, weaving together. Boys singing that a friend of theirs had lost his love, telling him he could win her back.

"Yeah, yeah, yeah." Flinging out the noise, "Oooo!" high and loud. Electric. A kind of howl, fierce, like — rebellion. My body swaying, head bouncing in time. Wild drums. Harmonies. Cascades of guitar.

They sounded — honest. Cheeky.

"You're not the hurting kind," they sang. I loved that. "Apologize to her," they sang. Apologize to her. What boy had ever said such a nice thing?

"Because she loves you," BANG, the music dipped, and then it climbed again. I had never listened so closely to a song. My heart was racing, beating in time.

"OOOOO!"

The call zinged through my body, charged my blood. Something new poured in. Courage. Glee.

"Yeah yeah yeah YEAH!"

A last note, pulsing in my chest. And it was over. Too fast.

Wow! Wow wow wow.

Frank Cameron was talking, but I couldn't hear. I was back on earth, heart pounding, pounding. Catching my breath. Oh yes. Oh yes yes yes. That was the way music should be — cheery and fresh and — free, that's what it was, it made me feel free too, and light, and ... raw, turned inside out. My body tingled. My stomach hurt. It felt like I'd been waiting for that sound, these feelings, and I'd woken up. As if my body and mind were a machine covered with dust that had just been switched on.

You know you should be glad, they said. I was *glad*.

I TWIRLED THE dial back to CBC, turned off the radio — that music was mine, my parents must never know what just happened — and rushed to call Lea, who'd been the biggest Beatle fan in class since way back in November. She was even growing out her fine blonde hair, which before was very short in a pixie cut. Now her bangs were drooping so close to her eyebrows that she'd received a warning from the headmistress. She was daring, fearless, was Lea.

"Lea, I heard them!" I said. "The Beatles. They're fantastic."

"Yeah, they're gear," she said.

"They're what?"

"It's a Beatle word," she said. "Their hair is gear their music is gear Liverpool is gear. It's about time you found out, Kaplan. But listen, there's another group you should hear too, called the Rolling Stones."

"Oh no," I said. "For me there is only one group from now until forever."

I lay on the floor of the hall closet under the coats, clutching the heavy black wall phone like a lifebuoy as Lea told me all about the Beatles, their names, their stories, the fact that one of them was married but the other three — what good news! — were not. We talked for two hours. It was the first time I'd talked all evening on the phone. The first time I didn't do my homework.

When my parents got back, stamping off the snow, Dad asked me how my evening had been.

"Gear," I said.

"What?" he said. He would never, ever understand.

In my room, I pretended to be in bed but was really setting my hair in bristle rollers with sticky pink Dippety-do like the big girls did. Tossing in pain that night, the bristles stabbing my skull, I crooned "Yeah yeah yeah" to myself, knowing that nothing would ever be the same. "Yeah yeah yeah YEAH."

Out in the hall, my parents were arguing. Something about Paris. Paris, France.

AT SCHOOL THE next morning, I walked right up to the main group of Beatlemaniacs — Sherry, Nancy, Louise, Marilyn, Sheila, Daphne, Kathy, Hillary, and, right in the middle, Lea — and interrupted. "God, they are so gear," I said. The circle parted, and I walked in.

Just like that, I had a crowd.

I could hardly believe how different it felt to belong, to be part of such an important cause. Until now, both at this private girls' school and at my previous school, the public one near my home, I had never had a crowd. I was good at school only by accident, so not one of the serious, hard-working teacher's pets; much too scaredy-cat to be a rule-breaking rebel, like Lea; on a different planet from the snooty, popular in crowd. The kooky outsiders, that's where I belonged. And we did not have a group, because we were outsiders.

But now I was a Beatlemaniac, and that was a very large crowd indeed. The two best things about being inside the magic circle: there was lots of company in there, and my mother and father were left outside, forever.

After school, Carol next door and I snuck to the Simpson's Shopping Centre, where I bought my first single, "She Loves You," of course, with "I'll Get You" on the other side, and two British fan magazines, one about George and one about John because the other two were sold out. The next day, draining my piggy bank, I bought "I Want to Hold Your Hand," another fab song with a Side B that was just as good, "I Saw Her Standing There." I played them a zillion times, softly, on my little pink record player, while memorizing everything about George and John. Like homework, only fun.

Carol lent me her brother Randy's old transistor, so I could listen secretly to the Hit Parade in my room. When the Beatles came on, I'd close my eyes and hold the transistor, almost as small as a deck of cards, right to my ear, listening to every breath, every chord. My folks thought I was doing homework! The two of them were so square, they were cubes. My dad played violin and viola in a string quartet with three of his scientist buddies, and my mother played the piano and every size of recorder in a recorder group and was learning the cello. The cello. They hated pop music. Daddy thought I should worship Mozart, like him. My mother wanted me to play the recorder, like her. Where did these people come from, Mars?

My parents wanted me to have cultural hobbies, but recently, except for piano, I'd quit all my extracurricular activities — ballet, Brownies and drama. At ballet, I was not good at doing exactly the same thing at exactly the same time as everyone else, which was, it seemed to me, the whole point of ballet.

At Brownies, Brown Owl and I did not see eye to eye. When she announced we were going to learn semaphore — the art of signalling on boats using coloured flags — I thought, if you're on a sinking boat, are you going to get out your little flags and figure out how to spell HELP, or are you going to jump up and down and yell?

I asked if I could please learn something else. That was the end of Brownies.

My parents thought acting was taking too much time away from school, although I was good at drama and had performed in two stage plays and on radio and a weekly children's program on local Halifax television. A boy recognized me on the bus once, and I felt like Marilyn Monroe. But I quit drama too.

Now my hobby was something my parents didn't even know about. All my free time would be spent with four boys from Liverpool. That was the best.

❦

BY THE END of January, I'd saved enough babysitting money to buy *Beatlemania! With the Beatles*, the first LP I'd ever bought. On the bus ride home, I clutched my shiny new album, those beautiful faces in half shadow, black and white, poring over every word on the cover: THE NEWSPAPERS SAY ... A NEW DISEASE IS SWEEPING THROUGH BRITAIN ... AND DOCTORS ARE POWERLESS TO STOP IT ... IT'S BEATLEMANIA!

How gear to have this disease. We all had it, my friends and I.

Everyone was out, so I didn't have to hide the album under my coat. In my room, I slipped the big black disc from its cover, placed it reverently on my little pink record player — remembering to switch the speed from 45 to 33 — and floated up to the ceiling, where I stayed. Seven songs on each side, one right after the other. So much Beatle.

A fantastic, upbeat song called "All My Loving" drove me wild, as I danced around my tiny bedroom. Bubbles of joy burst from my throat. But then, something different — the soft plinking of guitars with a quiet background thump, a lone voice so pure and husky, so angelic that my skin prickled and my throat clenched. I stopped dancing, stood swaying with my eyes closed, arms wrapped around my shoulders. Who was that? At the end, I wiped away tears and checked the cover, to be sure.

That was the voice for me. The boy for me.

It was Paul. Paul McCartney, the cute Beatle with the baby face, huge brown eyes with long curly eyelashes and soft, clear voice.

I put the song on again. The voice sang about birds in the sky ...

> *But I never sor them winging*
> *No I never sor them at all*
> *Till there was you.*

That Liverpool accent. I felt my body melting. Oooooh.
PAUL.

I had just made the most important decision every kid my age had to make: which Beatle? Of four fab boys, which one to love most? Lea had chosen John. I liked John too, he was handsome and funny, but there was something heavy about him, sharp. Anyway, he was married, there was no point liking him. Marilyn liked George, and sure, he was good-looking and sweet, but he was too quiet, kind of invisible. And as for goofy little big-nosed Ringo — well, someone somewhere must love Ringo, but I could not see why.

Paul — the soft-voiced balladeer and songwriter with big

down-sloping eyes, thick eyelashes, pouty mouth, chubby cheeks and baby face, perfect sense of humour, perfect clothes and hair and face and voice. Especially that clear, sweet voice. Especially everything.

I worshipped all four, the greatest group in the history of the world. But one of them was by far the best.

I was, and I would always be, a Paul Girl.

2

※

February

One cold morning, when I came down for breakfast, I was shocked to see that a kitchen window was broken and patched over; my mother was sweeping up glass, going on about Dad. My parents had gone out the night before to a faculty party, Mum all dressed up in her sparkly skirt, red lipstick and perfume, Dad for once wearing a tie. He'd drunk too much and was nasty to her, she said, so she'd driven home without him and locked the front door, and when he got home later, he'd broken the window to get in.

I felt sick. It was terrifying when they fought like that. But at least Mum hadn't woken me up. Sometimes, when she and Dad had a fight, she left their bedroom, came across the hall to mine and woke me up by climbing into my bed. It was nice that my mother found comfort with me, but secretly, I wished she would go somewhere else; I had enough trouble falling asleep without my giant crying mother. As I lay squashed against the wall, she'd whisper and weep about Dad — that he was clueless about money, that he insulted her at parties. I wanted to comfort her. I wanted her to be strong and go away. I didn't know what to do.

Though my mother was six feet tall, she was scared of

everything. Petrified. One night when I was eleven, she woke me up. Dad was away at a conference. "I heard a noise downstairs!" she whispered, clutching her bathrobe, her face white, eyes huge. "I'm sure someone has broken in."

We stood huddled in the upstairs hall, listening. I couldn't hear anything.

"Should we call the police?" I whispered.

"We can't wait that long," she said, gazing intently at me.

"Do you want me to go see?"

"Oh, would you?" Her face collapsed with relief. "That would be marvellous."

I tiptoed into Dave's bedroom — luckily he was still asleep — and grabbed a fat red plastic baseball bat. Holding the bat high in front of me, my heart thudding so loudly I thought the sound would shake the walls, I descended the stairs slowly, one by one. Down into the shadows of our sleeping house, looking, listening for the burglar. There was no one on the main floor. I opened the basement door and listened, though there was no way I was going to go down there. Even in daytime, the cobwebby basement was to be avoided at all costs. Nothing.

Mum hugged and kissed me gratefully — "What would I do without you, you brave thing?" — and went back to sleep. I stayed awake, listening to the house creak and rustle. The next day, she went to a store that sold records, asked the salesman what hit was popular with the kids and bought me the single "Save the Last Dance for Me" by the Drifters. We put it on the record player and laughed, because neither of us liked it much.

She'd tried though. That's how sweet she could be. I loved her very much. But I wanted her to leave me alone.

THE INCREDIBLE NEWS took the roof off the school: the Beatles were going to appear on *The Ed Sullivan Show*. I squealed with the others. And then the pathetic reality of my life: my family did not own a television set. My father called TV "the idiot box." "Pablum for the brain." "The opiate of the masses." When my friends at school discussed the great shows they were watching — *Leave it to Beaver, Dr. Kildare* or *Ben Casey* — unless I'd been able to watch on my neighbour Carol's idiot box, I had to pretend I knew what they were talking about.

Once this had backfired. I forgot that Brenda, my enemy in grade six at my old school, knew we didn't have a television, and one day as I hovered close, eavesdropping on her in-crowd circle, I heard Brenda loudly discussing a great TV show about the *Titanic*. Suddenly, she turned to me.

"Did you see it, Elizabeth?" she asked. I was shocked; she never included me.

"Sure, yes, I did," I said, sounding, I hoped, casual. "It was really good."

"That's so strange," she said with a smirk. "There *was* no program about the *Titanic*." And she and the others burst out laughing.

Was my face red.

From then on, I did not fib about seeing programs.

Occasionally, though, when there was something political or scientific he wanted to watch, like at election time, Dad rented a TV. Dave and I would cram in as much viewing as allowed — *Lassie*! *Zorro*! *I Love Lucy*! — before the television was sent back. And by some miracle, a few days before *Ed Sullivan*, a small set appeared in our dining room. Did Dad know how urgently I wanted to see the program? Surely not. He disapproved of the Beatles with every fibre of his being, and he didn't think much of Ed Sullivan either, except when there was classical stuff on, like Victor Borge.

And yet, there it was. A beautiful little TV.

AT SUPPERTIME ON Thursday, when it looked like Dad was full and maybe in a good mood, I said, "The Beatles are going to be on Ed Sullivan on Sunday and I'd like to watch please."

The fantasy: my parents smiling and saying, "By all means, dear, this new musical group is a fine one. The three of us will go far away and leave you to enjoy the show in peace."

"Surely you're not a fan of that crap," said my father. Tonight we were confronting my British mother's idea of hamburgers — hockey pucks on buns, with lettuce.

"I certainly am," I replied. "They're gear."

"What is that word you keep saying?" he barked.

"It means 'fantastic.'"

My brother sat eating every bit of his rubber burger. He always ate every single thing on his plate. For sure, he did it to make me look bad.

"Let's watch, Gord," said my mother. "It sounds like fun." And Dad said, "All right." He said all right. Did I hear correctly?

BACK IN MY room, I sighed at the homework stacked up on the desk, including an English assignment due the next day. English composition had always been my best subject, because writing was my favourite pastime. But now the topics were so dreary.

> Pick one of:
> — *a winter wonderland*
> — *my favourite sporting activity*
> — *a respected relative.*

I mean, come on. I picked up my pen. *My favourite sporting activity*, I wrote, *is running, laughing, through a meadow of wildflowers, hand in hand with my boyfriend Paul McCartney.*

No, Miss Salton would not be amused. I put on a record and took out a sheet of the good writing paper my American grandmother had given me for Christmas, with my name and address in swirly printing at the top.

Feb. 6 1964

Dear Paul:

I guess I have no real hope of you ever reading or answering this, because I'm nobody but a fan to you. It's hard for me to realize that you don't know I'm me — sitting in my messy room, surrounded by Beatle pictures, listening to "She Loves You."

Paul, you are married to me and about sixty other girls in our school alone. (In case you didn't know.) We have two kids — Paul Junior and Paula — and we live in a ranch with a wood floor and a big fireplace. I've imagined so much, down to the minutest detail! I'm telling you this because I know you'll never know me. We did a poll on you in our class, and you won by a large marjority — Ringo next, then George, then poor John. I think it is because he is married, you know. I mean, really married! Not like you.

Paul, you really don't shave enough. I know I sound frightfully cheeky, but it shoes in nearly all the pictures. Sorry to be so awful. You know we love you.

I hope you can answer this letter! Anything you write will do! I've just sat down and wrote as I would speak. Good luck, keep bouncing.

> *Love*
> *Beatlebeth.*

P.S. In reading this letter over, it makes me sound like an idiot. Well, I am an idiot.

Then I read in 16 magazine that the thing Paul hated most was shaving. So I was relieved I hadn't sent the letter and upset him with my criticism. Before my dad shaved, he liked to give me "whisker rubs," scraping his sharp prickles over my cheeks, and though he made me squeal with laughter, afterwards my face was red and sore. But Paul's prickles would be gentle. And anyway, I'd get used to them.

SUNDAY, FEBRUARY 9, was Beatleday. In the afternoon, Dave and I were allowed to watch the Olympics and jumped up and down when Canada actually won a gold medal. All that day, I was praying my family would just go somewhere, vanish, before 8 o'clock. But no — after dinner, my mother moved the TV to the living room, "a better spot for family viewing." Groan. I was on the floor, two inches in front of the set, by 7:30. At 8 the rest of them, my habitual panel of judges and jury, were sitting on the sofa behind me, getting ready to laugh. "We want to see what all the fuss is about," said Dad.

I was trembling. When Ed Sullivan said something about New York never having witnessed such excitement before, I wanted to turn around and stick out my tongue. See?

And when he said, "Ladies and gentlemen, the Beatles!" and the kids in the audience started screaming, I thought my heart would burst right out of my body. Oh how I wanted to be there with those lucky kids, to vanish into Beatleworld forever.

"Christ," said a voice behind me. "Banshees."

There they were in person, the first time I'd seen their whole bodies, their legs skinny in tight black pants, wearing matching black jackets and white shirts and black ties, their hair shiny and perfect and so very *long*. I wanted to scream like the audience, my heart was hammering, they started with "All My Loving," my favourite, they grinned and looked happy and girls were crying,

George leaning in and out to the microphone, Ringo bashing away at the back, tossing his head — though I hardly saw those two, the background ones. In front was tall John Lennon with his legs planted wide. And singing away on the other side, his head bobbing and a grin on his face, was the most beautiful boy in the universe.

The song was over too soon, they bowed, lots of ear-splitting screaming, and then they started — I knew it like my own heartbeat — "Till There Was You." Oh Paul — that angel face, that gentle voice that went right through the whole length of my body and made me shiver.

When they launched into "She Loves You," I thought I would faint. At the "OOO" part, Paul and George WAGGLED THEIR HEADS. Heart-stopping. If only I didn't have to listen to my father, who whenever the "oooo" came up, howled at the top of his lungs. Watching them was paradise, but it was also hell. I wasn't backstage in New York waiting for my boyfriend Paul to finish so we could go somewhere private and romantic. I was thirteen and didn't know them, I was in my living room in Halifax Nova Scotia, and behind me was my father, baying like a wolf.

The first half ended. I was a melted pool of girl, music seeping from my skin.

"Barbarians at the gate," said Dad. "The mating call of wild dogs."

"They're much too loud," said Mum, "but I think they're rather sweet. Don't you, Beth?"

Rather sweet? Those boys who meant more than breathing? I slid out to call Lea, who was hysterical.

"Fab suits!" she squealed. "John is mine. I hated that 'Sorry girls he's married' thing."

"Paul's a living doll!" I said. "Eyelashes a foot long!"

Back for the second half. Mr. Sullivan said they'd received a wire from Elvis Presley welcoming them to this country, and that they'd be on again the following Sunday in a show starring "the exciting Mitzi Gaynor," whoever that was. They sang "I Saw Her Standing There." Oh Paul, I wanted to cry, I'll be seventeen in only four years, will you see *me* standing there?

And then "I Want to Hold Your Hand." There was a shot of a grown woman, at least twenty-five, screaming like the kids. Then the Fab Four were standing smiling beside Ed Sullivan, shaking his hand like real people. It was the most wonderful sight I had ever seen. And then it was over.

"They're Neanderthals, with all that hair," said Dad, switching off the TV. "And you're a Neanderthal for liking such nonsense."

"Actually," said my mother, "I thought they were lovely."

Oh great, I thought, now they're going to fight about the Beatles. I said I had homework so I could run to my room and dream. Dream dream dream.

BY THE NEXT week, on the Hit Parade, the Beatles had number 1, 2, 3, 5 and 9. Poor old Ricky Nelson's "For You" was #10. Why bother, Ricky? I thought. Only the moptops counted. They were on *Ed Sullivan* again the next Sunday, and the next. The show on February 16 from Miami wasn't as good, and Dad was so critical — he said they were hairy apes and I was a pathetic moron — he made me cry. But Ed Sullivan was sweet. He told us that their first show had "played to the greatest TV audience that's ever been assembled in the history of American TV." And he called them "four of the nicest youngsters we've ever had on our stage." No kidding.

The one on February 23 was spectacular, because my family did go out; I got to watch it alone and scream all by myself. How I loved Mr. Sullivan. "Their conduct over here," he said, "not only as fine professional singers but as a group of fine youngsters, will leave an imprint on everyone who's met them."

I knew the exact words because they were quoted in the newspapers. The stories said more than seventy-three million people had watched the first show, and while they were on, there was almost no crime anywhere in the United States. But did my father, who read all the newspapers, read the bit about fine youngsters and no crime? Obviously not.

I expressed the fever of my soul in a new blue notebook.

WHAT IS PAUL?

Paul is a misty dream
A whispering shadow
A glowing thought
Paul is an ache in my heart
A lonely sigh
A daydream saught
Paul ... Paul ... Paul ...

"A lonely sigh ... so romantic and true," sighed Lorna at school, after reading my poem. She showed me the pictures of Paul in her binder. It was all very well, those other girls loving him, but I hoped they realized he was mine.

Real boys were scary and confusing. Paul was different.

🜚

TWO WEEKS LATER, at suppertime, Dad shifted the shepherd's pie around in his mouth and took a swig of wine. "So, kids," he said. "I've got a big surprise for you."

Oh no, I thought. My father's surprises were mostly hard or boring — meeting foreigners, visiting scientists or men of peace whose English was hard to understand — or tickets to museums or classical concerts. Educational things that were good for us, at least according to him.

He had that kind of light in his eyes now. My little brother David, too, put down his fork and waited. My mother looked at her plate.

"We're going to spend all next year," he said, "in Paree! Paris, France."

What? Where?

Dad told us that as a university professor, he was granted a year off with half salary every seven years; it was called, he explained, a sabbatical. I knew what the word meant. I'd not forgotten the last sabbatical seven years ago, when he'd carted us over to freeze to death in my mother's hometown of London, England. The worst time of my life. Now, in July, he told us, we'd be sailing over to spend a whole year in France.

"I want you kids to learn fluent French like mine," said Dad.

My father was mad for France. We'd heard a million times how he landed in Paris during the war with his U.S. Army regiment and became their translator. How he fell in love with wine, women and song. He was always singing dirty French songs with forty choruses, especially the one about dying with his head under the tap of a wine barrel. Now he'd be able to give that a try.

I hated him.

My mother smiled weakly. "It'll be a marvellous adventure, kids," she said. "You'll see."

Who cared about learning French like his? I did not want to be anything like him, ever. And I wanted to stay right where I was.

"But where'll we live, Dad?" asked David, who was nine. My brother and Dad were as close as could be. I hated my sucky brother too.

"My friend Jacques has found us an apartment in the same

building as his, and I've found schools for you. Dave's is around the corner, and you, Beth, will go to a ..." — he said something in French — "a new kind of French high school. They agreed to take you, though your math marks are weak. We'll do remedial geometry over the summer."

Remedial. Geometry.

"So what do you think?" he asked, grinning at me. "Exciting, no?"

Trying to stop my voice from wobbling, I said, "I don't want to go to Paris. I want to stay here."

"You'll love it," he said. "Pass the shepherd's pie, Syl."

"You'll love it, Beth," said my mother with that look on her face. How did she create that look, supporting my father and at the same time full of sympathy for me? It was a talent she had, my mum, making everyone think she was on their side.

Desperation made me brave. "What if we don't want to go?" I said.

My father's eyes hardened into black stones. "You'll go," he said, in his one-more-minute-and-here-comes-a-smack voice.

Hot water in my eyes. I blinked fast to stop it.

"Now Gord," said my mother, "tell them the nice things about the trip."

Nice? Being dragged away from everything you love?

"We're sailing over from New York," Dad said, "on the SS France — a luxury ocean liner with a movie theatre and swimming pools. And the food!" Shovelling more in. "I'm going on a diet right now, because the food is delicious and all paid for in advance, so you can eat as much as you want."

Joy.

AS SOON AS the dishes were done, which David never had to help with because he was a boy, I fled to my room, shut the door and fell on the bed to weep. This was not new, my dad getting wild ideas and dragging the rest of us along — no discussion, no complaints, his great scientific brain made a decision, and that was that. But an entire year away was extreme, even for him.

How did parents just get to ruin your life? And why now? How could he wreck everything now? Finally, I had friends and music. And best of all, I had love. Real true love, with the handsomest kindest boy on earth.

He was waiting for me in my room. Of course he was, now that I needed him so. As I listened to his tender voice and felt his soft arms tight around me, I wanted to believe that not even my father, my direst enemy, could hurt me when there was love like this to keep me safe.

I got up to put the record on again. One day I just might wear "Till There Was You" right out. The guitar and drums started, and I sank back onto my bed, pressing the album cover to my chest. My boyfriend, the love of my life, crooning this ballad just for me.

There was a stack of homework on my desk, a big English assignment on *Ivanhoe*. No time for *Ivanhoe*. There was only music and love.

Music. Love. Music.

Paul.

I SNUCK INTO the hall closet to call my fellow Paul Girl, small ferocious Hillary, and tell her the horrible news, that in the summer I'd be torn away from home to a strange place where I didn't speak the language and had no friends, and where there would be no Frank Cameron's Hit Parade and probably no peanut butter.

"Elizabeth," she said — Hillary was the only one who still called me Elizabeth — "you stupid dummy, are you nuts? What is France close to?"

"What?"

"ENGLAND, you idiot! You'll be right next door — on the right side of the pond. Maybe you'll *meet* them."

I considered this possibility. But miracles only happened in books, like to Sara Crewe in my favourite book, *A Little Princess*. They did not happen to me.

I DECIDED JUST to forget about our trip to France. It simply could not, would not happen. The last trip — the one to England — had been bad.

I lay on my bed, and though I tried not to, I remembered.

3

July 1956

We sailed from Halifax just before my sixth birthday, and moved into a rented house in Golders Green, in north London. We were still settling in when a visitor arrived — Daddy's good friend Charles, also a scientist at Dalhousie. A few days later, my dad went away to a scientific conference in Brussels. "Look after my family for me, old chap," he said, slapping his friend on the back.

The next morning, Charles pulled up to our front door in a dark green car with a silver cat on the hood. Mummy put a letter addressed to Daddy on the mantelpiece. "We're going on a little trip," she told us, her face strange. "With Charles."

As we drove, I could see from the back seat that Charles and my mother were touching each other's hands. "You two are sitting too close," I said.

Mum turned around. "Beth, dear," she said, "Charles is taking us to a marvellous place. He loves you and David a lot."

I didn't want him to love me a lot. I had a father to love me a lot. We stopped at a hotel by the seaside, and Charles bought shiny buckets and spades so we could play in the sand. David was having fun. But I didn't understand why Mummy whispered and laughed so with Charles. She slept in the room with Dave and me, but late one night, before I fell asleep, she tiptoed out. In the morning, she was there again.

After three days, my brother started to call Charles "Daddy."

"He's not our daddy," I shouted. "We already have a daddy."

Where was our father? My mother looked happy and sad at the same time. Even though he was being nice to us, I did not like Charles.

THE FOUR OF us were eating breakfast in the hotel dining room when the door flew open and there was my father. His face was red. Charles stood up; his face was white.

"How dare you?" said my father. And then he said in a loud voice that Charles was trying to steal his family. Charles said he was terribly sorry, but my mother had chosen him.

"Is that true, Sylv?" said my dad. "Is what he says true?"

My mother started to cry great floods of tears. David started to cry too, and so did I. Everyone else in the dining room went on drinking tea and eating toast as if nothing was happening.

"That's enough, Sylv, we're getting out of here," Daddy said.

We walked to the car and drove all the way back to Golders Green, my mother wiping her eyes, my father silent.

When we pulled up outside the house, the green car with the silver cat was parked there already, Charles sitting behind the wheel, looking at us. My mother burst into sobs. My father turned away from her.

"Go to him then," he said.

Mummy opened the door. She got out, crossed the street, over to where Charles was, and got in. The big car drove away. My father and I sat, looking at nothing. My brother was asleep. Daddy woke him up and carried him into the cold dark house, explaining that Mummy had gone away for a while. I helped him find Dave's clean pyjamas. In my own bed, I could not stop shivering.

MY FATHER HAD to go to work, so he hired a housekeeper, Mrs. Wilcox. She and I were alone in the house — Dave was at nursery school — and I was reading Enid Blyton's exciting "Go Ahead, Secret Seven," when the doorbell rang. Mrs. Wilcox opened the door. It was Mummy. I ran and threw my arms around her. She picked me up. I could feel her trembling.

"Now, ma'am," said Mrs. Wilcox, "Dr. K. says that nobody is allowed ..."

My mother turned with me in her arms and walked out to the street. She carried me around the corner, tight in her arms, and there was Charles, waiting in the car.

Now I had a mother but no father. The two of us lived with Grandma and Grandpa Leadbeater, Mum's parents, though my mother disappeared sometimes; Charles was living nearby. It was as if my mother owned me now, and David belonged to Dad. They came over to visit one Sunday afternoon. I didn't know if I was allowed to hug Daddy or not, but he held me in his arms for a minute, and I held him really hard back, smelling his pipe tobacco smell. My parents drank tea and tried to talk.

David did not want to leave. It hurt to hear my brother howl as the door closed behind them.

NEARLY TWO MONTHS later, I came home from my new school to find my mother dissolved in sobbing. The boss at Dalhousie had found Charles a job at another university on the other side of Canada. Though he didn't want to, Charles was sailing back to his own wife and children. I was overjoyed. My mother was heartbroken. But she said she'd realized that, because of us, she would always have my father in her life.

"He's impossible, Beth. But he's also a marvellous man, and I do love him."

That weekend was my mother's thirty-third birthday, and thirty-three white roses arrived at the flat from Charles. There were vases everywhere, and many, many tears.

IT TOOK A long time, but in January 1957 we all moved into the second floor of an old farmhouse in Mill Hill, near Dad's lab. My parents had their room, and Dave and I had our room. We were all in one place again.

I started at Frith Manor School. It was the middle of the year so a bit confusing, but Miss Price helped me sort myself out. My mother left early every morning to go to her own school. Charles, she told me, had urged her to get a social work degree, and she was excited to have been accepted at the London School of Economics since she hadn't even finished grammar school because of the war. But I hated anything to do with Charles.

Things at home were much better. And yet perhaps they weren't. One night when a colleague of Dad's was there for dinner, there was a lot of noise in the kitchen, my parents arguing. With my brother sleeping nearby, I lay on my cot with the wet rolling down into my ears. The dinner guest came in, a scientist from South Africa called Vimpy.

"A bit upset, are we?" Vimpy said, stroking my hair. "Here's some advice my mother gave me." He leaned in closer. "When you cry, don't ever blow your nose or rub your eyes. It'll make your nose and eyes red and swollen. Just dab, like this." And he took out his handkerchief and carefully patted my eyes and nose, until they were dry. He made me smile. "See? Then no one will know you've been crying."

I wondered if he had given this kind advice to my mother.

A FEW MONTHS after my seventh birthday, Daddy had to return to his lab in Halifax. But Mum wanted to finish her social work program, so we would come to join him at the end of next year's spring term. At least I hoped we would. My mother said she would only come back to Halifax if Dad bought us our own house.

He left sadly, all alone.

I wrote poems and stories. My first long story was about a little girl who lived in an eight-room mud hut with her fluffy white kitten, whose name was Fluffy. And I sent Dad my first letter, in the wonderful cursive writing we were learning at school.

> ... *Have you learnt Canadyan? Please wright back and tell me all the exsighting news about Canada. It would be nice to hear news since I am satch along way of from you.*
> *GOODBYE DEAR DADDY, love Beth. P.T.O.*
> *I loved the letter you sent me with the very sad Dad on it.*
> *I DID IT ALL MY SELF.*

Daddy wrote that he'd put a down payment on a house, our first house, with a big garden especially for Mum. She was nervous — what if she didn't like it? But he was sure she would.

I wished my father were around, to cheer us up with his jokes.

MUMMY, DAVID AND I sailed back to Halifax in July 1958, two years after we'd left and a month before my eighth birthday. As our boat was docking in St. John's, Newfoundland, I wanted us all to go up and look at Canada, but my mother lay curled up on her bed in our cabin, weeping. I took David's hand, and we went up on deck to see if we could find our father. There he was, standing with the crowd on shore, waving his arms wildly. We stood waving back, waving.

After the gangplank went down, ship officials announced that no one would be allowed to board yet. My little brother and I stood watching as Daddy tried to push his way up the gangplank. A man in a uniform had to pull him back. "You'll have to wait, sir, like everyone else," he said.

"Those are my children!" my father shouted, as he struggled to free himself. "I want my children!"

"They're hurting Daddy," David cried and wanted to run over to fight. I held him back. When they finally let the crowd board, our father rushed up the gangplank and grabbed us in his arms.

"Where is your mother?" he said.

We led him down to the cabin. Mummy had put on lipstick. She looked pretty. My parents hugged.

OUR OWN HOUSE was perfect, on a wide street leading to Point Pleasant Park. My mother looked happier than she had for a long time, and my father too.

But I knew now that parents could just disappear. I knew how fragile our family really was, how easily we could break apart.

It was my job to make sure that we didn't.

4

❧

March

So, on top of my many day-to-day anxieties — pimples, exams, flat chest, messy room, unstylish clothes — I was preoccupied with the upcoming trip. First, we'd visit my father's parents and the rest of his big family in New York, then sail across the Atlantic to England to visit my mother's parents in London, and then to Paris. I wasn't afraid the same thing would happen as last time. But we were going to live for a whole year far from everything familiar, in a place where, without friends nearby, I'd be at the mercy of my mother and father, the most complicated, confusing, sometimes hurtful people on earth.

They taught us in school about Cassandra, a Greek goddess whose fate was to see danger coming but to have her warnings be ignored. As soon as I heard that story, I knew I was Cassandra Kaplan of 816 Young Avenue, Halifax, Nova Scotia. It was my fate to see the disaster we were as a family but to cry out in vain. My parents resented each other, and I resented them and also my brother and he resented me. Even the poor dog got into trouble — when she had an accident on the floor, Dad whacked her with a rolled-up newspaper. But the worst was my father and me.

For some reason, my father didn't like me now. *I'm sure Daddy hates me*, I wrote in my diary. *He shows as much in words and deeds.*

He loved his son way too much and his daughter not nearly enough, that's just the way it was, and there didn't seem to be anything I could do about it except duck fast when a smack was coming my way.

All fathers were like my dad, the rulers of their families, expected to punish kids — and dogs — when punishment was necessary. Their authority was never questioned. I felt lucky that, though he whacked us both, Dad had given me only one brief spanking, and Dave one or two. I just kept as far beyond his reach as possible.

But I could not avoid his critical words. He said I was spoiled, selfish and lazy, a list of flaws I'd heard so often it was like one word: spoiledselfishlazy. He corrected my bad posture, my sibilant "s," my nervous habits. Dad had made clear that he'd prefer a more interesting daughter. I could see her, a tomboy, a fearless tree-climbing girl with a long braid down her back who wore dungarees and played with trucks. She loved exotic food and humming along to Mozart and didn't care what anyone thought except, of course, him.

Whereas I liked dresses and dolls, hated all food except peanut butter and white chicken and cared very much what others thought. I was ordinary — a conformist, a disappointment, a daughter like other daughters. If only I were the unconventional girl my father wanted. "Oh Daddy," she'd cry, her eyes shining, "my dream come true! A whole year in Paris with you!"

"My precious girl," he'd say. And they'd hug.

Definitely not my story.

AS FOR MY mother — I knew she loved me. She loved everyone. But she was critical too, always fussing, and I never knew where I stood. When she was miserable, she wanted to climb into bed with me, and I always felt I wasn't doing enough to make things right for her. Mum was like a nice hot bath that could suddenly turn cold. My father was a volcano ready to erupt.

When unhappiness overwhelmed me, I fell into a black hole from which there was no escape. I thought of home as a prison pit, sure they didn't want me there, and I wanted to run away. But where would I go? A page at the back of my current one-year diary was witness to my despair.

There are 2 things I could do.
a. Try to escape from the pit.
b. Commit suicide.

1. I sometimes try to keep away from the prison pit as long as possible. But the guards just yank the chain and back I go. Keep trying.

As for no. 2, the guards and the abominable other prisoner are driving me to it. I'm sure heaven isn't a prison, God a nagging, unreasonable guard.

But then a special letter would arrive to raise my spirits. I had written to my British grandparents, asking them to send anything Beatle, and to my pen pal Babs too — *You live right there in England, you lucky stiff!* Envelopes stuffed with pictures neatly cut out of British magazines and newspapers began dropping through the front door. Babs sent not only the Fab Four but Gerry and the Pacemakers and other British dreamboats like Billy J. Kramer and Cliff Richard. By mistake, she sent me the Dave Clark Five. I ripped those up and wrote back to tell her how much I hated them, that they were Beatles imitators, fake and ugly and not worth anything at all. Babs apologized immediately. She agreed.

I proudly brought my precious stash of pictures to school, to show everyone — direct from England, the latest, no one else had them — and was the envy of the class for a bit, until someone else came in with new pictures. Then I stuck mine on my walls; the Twenty Wildflowers in my room vanished, taped over with photographs. Any problem could be made better by gazing at my walls. One look at the Beatles at the Cavern Club in Liverpool or clowning around in a swimming pool in Florida — you could almost see their bare chests — and my sore heart lifted.

I sharpened my coloured pencils and drew my own pictures of the four moptops, and started trying to grow and comb my hair like Lea's so it fell over my forehead. Not too long though; kids were getting thrown out of school for that. I spent hours sticking pictures into my new Beatles scrapbook.

And round and round on the little pink record player went my precious LP and my singles with the yellow and orange swirls at the centre. I saved my allowance to buy two more, "Please Please Me/From Me to You" and "Love Me Do/P.S. I Love You." Music that lived inside me, that was never out of my head. Round and round and round.

Sometimes a song hit me so hard, I had to lift the needle and sit in silence, tears running down. The melody moved into my body, travelled through every bit of me. I wasn't just listening to the music. I was the music.

P.S. I love you. You you you. You you you. I love you.

FOR THE FIRST time, the teachers were mad at me. I'd always been a good student, but now I hadn't done the "Rime of the Ancient Mariner" homework. I'd lost my hideous puffy blue gym bloomers and my American history textbook and got my Latin declensions wrong — amo, amas, amat, ama — what? We love what? Of all the things to forget, how could I forget "we love"?

I hardly knew who I was any more, so restless they made me move to the front of the class so the teachers could keep an eye on me. My mother and I argued every day about listening to the radio and not practicing the piano or doing my homework.

March 13

Had to come again and write lines for Mrs. Joyce. Mrs. Corston gave me a mag containing 3 pictures of the Beatles!!! Joy. Was going to go to Lea's tomorrow but of course Mum said no. She was mad because I didn't finish the dishes. To hell with her.

I had never spoken that way about my mother, even to myself, let alone on paper. To hell with her. The daring new me.

The telephone was the third most important device in the world after the record player and the transistor. In the evening, I'd tiptoe into the hall closet, close the big wooden door behind me and lie for hours on the floor under the coats, stretching the black cord to its end, chatting to Lea and anyone else who would talk about the Beatles, also about clothes and hair and boys but mostly Beatles.

My mother discovered me there one night; she nearly stepped on me when she went to get something from her coat. "Get up!" she shouted. "No more jabbering on the phone." I stomped off to my room and slammed the door, but I knew she was too distracted by her own life to remember for long what she'd decreed about mine. And then she told me the TV was being sent back because my homework was suffering. My homework was suffering. What about MY suffering? I hated her.

I got out my blue story notebook and the Beatles fan magazine I was reading, and wrote a little scene, for consolation.

"Paul McCartney is the most beautiful Beatle. What affects people about Paul is his eyes, as sweet and innocent as an angel's. He is every parent's boy, bright, eager and receptive. He is also very intelligent."

Paul and I laughed over this magazine as we sat, sunk in plush chairs, toasting marshmallows by the flickering firelight.

"So, he thinks I'm beautiful? He's right, y'know." He cocked his head and fluttered his eyelashes. "D'you think I'm beautiful?

"Oh, definitely," I laughed, "my bright, eager, intelligent boy."

"I am, definitely," he said, grinning at me. "I'm fascinating. I could study me for hours and all."

Oh my sweet Paul, I thought, scooping up our dachshund who was asleep on my bed, squeezing her tight and covering her head with kisses. So could I.

MY BEATLE COLLECTION was growing; I tabulated in my diary that I had *over one hundred pictures and more articles, 1 LP, 7 singles and also Beatle Books and a big pin*. Though that list was followed by a brief moment of doubt.

I am posed by a big question. Do I love them because of their looks, accents, singing and style, or is it because everybody else loves them?

The doubt passed. My heart was oh so true.

ONE APRIL MORNING, in the school bathroom, I stared at my underpants in horror. Then I remembered my mother pulling me onto her lap last year and delivering a talk about how becoming a woman meant blood, when you got something called the Curse. It had sounded terrifying, and I'd cried. But this must be it. I'd caught up with my schoolmates, who'd all started ages ago.

My first thought was, "Finally my breasts will grow!" They said that when menstruation started, your bust developed, and I was desperate for mine to start. In the fall, when my neighbour Carol found out I was the only girl in grade nine without a brassiere, she had insisted on taking me to the shopping centre to buy my first — 32AA, really an undershirt shaped like a bra, which on the ride home cut so deeply into my ribcage that it hurt to breathe. But I didn't mind. Maybe the others on the bus were noticing my shapely new shape.

Flat-chested girls never got a boyfriend. And also girls whose hair did not flip. Unless I slept in bristle rollers, which hurt all night long, my hair just would not turn up at the ends in the proper way. Surely getting my period would cause my unsatisfactory breasts and hair to do what they should.

I went to the office, called home and whispered my secret to Mum, asking her to come and get me. But when the Morris Minor pulled up in front, my father was at the wheel. I prayed Mum hadn't told him. Some chance. My mother did not know the meaning of the word "secret."

"My little Pupik," Dad said softly. Pupik was his favourite nickname for me, though I didn't know why; it meant "belly button" in Yiddish. When he was annoyed, he called me "Sarah Heartburn, the Tragic Queen." Oh what a clever name. So amusing.

"My Pupikina, now capable of reproduction," he said, patting me on the knee. "Ah, the miracle of genetic continuity."

As usual, I had no idea what he was talking about. If only sometimes he would speak English.

My mother showed me how to hook a bulky pad onto an elastic strap thing around my waist, like a grown-up diaper, and then I had to lie down with a hot water bottle on my stomach. As I'd learned with rollers, growing up meant bother and pain. Now I was a woman, and it hurt.

Which was not a surprise. Being a woman had never looked that good to me. Women were second best. Boys had more freedom and fun, more choices, more muscles, way fewer boring chores. They were good at math, science and sports; girls weren't. I didn't know why that was so, but it was. Yet I knew I was just as good as boys in some ways — not at sports or math, nowhere near, but at English, writing, acting, at watching the world and figuring it out.

I'd heard a teacher say that educating girls was a waste of time. It didn't matter what they learned in school; they were only going to get married and stop whatever they were doing to raise children. I knew I'd never get married and have children, at least, until I met Paul.

But now I too was capable of reproduction. My body had made me join the big girls' club of pain. But despite the bother and cramps, despite that awkward thing between my legs, I was glad to have the Curse. I wanted to join.

The best thing about this messy business, besides the fact that my bust line would develop, was that now I had a good excuse to miss gym.

DADDY TOLD US he was advertising through university channels for a family to rent our house for a year. So he was going ahead with his horrible plan. In my diary, I listed all the positive French things I could think of: *Christian Dior perfume, gorgeous men, long sticks of bread.* That was it. When the girls at school heard why I might not be at school with them the following year, some of them said, "You're so lucky — Paris!"

"Well, you go then," I replied.

In Mrs. Ryan's art appreciation class, we happened to be studying great works from the Louvre — the *Mona Lisa,* the *Venus de Milo,* the whole bit — so I paid more attention than I usually would, and in French class too. But I hung onto the thought that it was just not possible this dreaded exile would take place.

Mum barged into my room one evening and discovered my LP. I thought she was going to yell. But "Till There Was You" was playing, and she actually stood and listened.

"I have to admit — it's melodic," she said.

"That's Paul," I said. "He's my favourite."

"I can see why," she said.

Sometimes grown-ups amazed you.

EVERY CHRISTMAS, I got books from my parents. The Christmas before last, I'd ripped off the wrapping paper to find the book every twelve-year-old wants to read: *Paderewski: Pianist and Patriot.* Gosh, Dad, this biography of a dead Polish pianist was at the top of my Christmas list, thanks! That same year, though, he also gave me *Don't Knock the Corners Off,* a real published book by a girl who was only fifteen. And he always gave me a *Mad* magazine, one of my favourite things. Sometimes they got it right.

On Easter weekend, I finally got around to the book they'd given me for Christmas. I read *The Diary of Anne Frank.*

I'd heard of her, of course. I knew she was a Jewish girl who'd hidden from the Nazis and had died in a concentration camp just before the war ended, which was not even twenty years ago. What I didn't know was that she was a great, great writer. There she was, in mortal danger, writing with such vivid intensity and purpose about her life. I'd read a lot of books, but her diary was the best. It made me feel like I knew her — in some ways, that I *was* her. Anne's anger at parents who didn't understand her, her love of writing and sense of herself as alone, unheard, unappreciated — it was all me.

As the end of the book approached, so did my dread. It was not possible that someone so gifted, sensitive and smart would be taken away to die. A girl just my age when the diary began, only two years older at the end, taken away to die. But she was. I knew that was how the story ended, but I willed it not to. When I came to the final page, I put the book down and wailed.

How could people be so monstrously cruel, life so unfair? I could not stop crying. Part of my pain was the thought that I too, though only half-Jewish, I too and all my family would have been hunted down with hatred, just like Anne.

With my eyes nearly swollen shut, I went to tell my dad what I was feeling. He was Jewish. He'd understand.

Dad reached to the top of his bookshelf and took down a big book of photographs. "Hard to fathom what humanity's capable of, Pupik," he said. "We must never forget. Six million."

They were pictures taken inside a concentration camp. After three pages I thought I would be sick, and after a few more, I ran back to my room, devastated now beyond tears. It was unbearable to think of any human being in a place like that, let alone idealistic Anne. A girl like me, in a place like that.

A darkness entered my soul, a new awareness of the black side of life. From then on, every time my heart was light, and I felt hopeful and happy — I'd remember the pictures in Dad's book and sink down to the cold, grey earth.

Luckily, the Beatles were there, singing away, to lift me back up.

THAT EASTER SUNDAY, I went as usual to church with my mother. Though Mum had been raised Church of England, she didn't really believe in anything at all. But for some reason she'd decided she and I should go to St. Paul's Anglican Cathedral every Sunday, though my brother didn't have to, and our going drove my father into a rage. He did not want me to believe in God; he thought people who believed in God were simpletons, with the exception of Albert Schweitzer. So every Sunday, while Mum and I put on our best coats, hats and gloves, Dad banged around the house, then took my brother somewhere special for the whole day.

I didn't care about religion; I just wanted to please my mother and join our neighbours, and maybe get revenge on my furious father by driving him a little nuts. But that Easter, sitting in the stuffy basement Sunday school room where we kids went to learn about Jesus and all that, I heard white-haired Mrs. Peabody say something about the infinite love of God for all his children. And rage flooded me.

"Excuse me, Mrs. Peabody," I said. "If God's love is so infinite, how do you explain the murder of six million Jews?"

The class froze. No one asked questions, and for sure nobody ever mentioned Jews. Mrs. Peabody stared at a point above my head, her pale eyes bulgy and watering.

"Well, Elizabeth," she said, still looking above me, "that's a very difficult question. It has to do with the whole nature of good and evil, which is far beyond what I can deal with here."

When Dad got home, after taking Dave to a restaurant and a movie and for ice cream, I told him what I'd said and that I did not want to go back. He looked at my mother in triumph. "Maybe a chip off the old block after all," he said. "Let me feel my bumps."

Dad had discovered that my head was square and had actual corners. When he was happy with me, he liked to squeeze the corners of my head.

Churchgoing with my mother was over.

ON MONDAY, I shut up in a box all my five-year and one-year diaries and walked to Stairs' Drugstore on Inglis Street. For a long time I stood in front of the scribbler section, looking at different sizes and kinds of paper and bindings before choosing an ordinary black spiral notebook with wide lines. That night I started a new kind of diary, with as many or as few lines as needed — limitless space for each day, thanks to Anne Frank, my guardian angel of writing.

And like Anne with her letters to her imaginary pen pal Kitty, my pages wouldn't be just to and for myself. I chose a kind older woman, Helen, who was eager to hear from me. From then on, I had a dear, close friend to talk to every single day, for as long as I wanted.

April 8, Wednesday, '64

Dear Helen:

I'm in a hurry to get this on paper! It'll sound stupid, childish and completely unbalanced, but I'm madly in love with Paul McCartney, a 21 year old man whom I have never seen in life (only in hundreds of photos) and don't know. Oh, he's tearing me apart inside! He's a Beatle, who I have preciously mentioned, but suddenly a passion has been awakened. Oh, Helen, I know — it's a teenage crush, like on a movie star. But I do love him so. Oh I love, love, love, love, love him.

I recently saw an article with a picture of his girlfriend — a 17 year old actress. And oh, how stupid I am to want him so. I mean, if I were a sexy 17 year old British actress, and he just happened to know me, then maybe I'd have cause to adore and desire him. But I'm just a 13 year old Canadian school-girl, nondescript in every way. So hopeless! And yet I adore him with all my heart. Oh, Paul, Paul, Paul.

April 8, Wednesday, '6[...]

Dear Helen:

I'm in a hurry to get this on paper. It'll sound stupid, childish and completely unbalanced, but I'm madly in love with Paul McCartney, a 21-year old man whom I have never seen in life (only in hundreds of photos), and don't know. Oh, Helen, he's tearing me apart inside! He's a Beatle, who I have previously mentioned, but suddenly a passion has been awakened. Oh, I know it's a teenage crush, like on a movie star. But I do love him so. Oh I love, love, love, love him. I recently saw an article with a picture of his girlfriend – a 17 year old actress. And oh, how stupid I am to want him so. I mean, if I were a

April 18, '64

Dear Helen:
I know now what it's like to be a teen. It's a muddling, confusing world — full of hates, loves, crushes, distractions and problems and counteracting conflicting emotions (e.g. right now I hate my mother and I love my mother.) I feel too passionately about the Beatles but I can't restrain myself. My school work is lagging. My mind roars at me. I cry a lot. My brain thinks five things at once and I can't concentrate on one. It's a world of doing things and regretting it, or not doing things and regretting it. I can't figure it out.

What can I do? Where can I go when I feel trapped by the whole world? To whom can I turn when my heart is overflowing with tears? Why is everybody so mean? How can I do homework when my life needs mending?

There is no answer to these questions and never will be. You must be filled with them, forever.

My father was always accusing me of being melodramatic. Who wouldn't be, when life was so hard to understand?

5

May

My English teacher, Miss Salton, looked at me sadly. She was skinny and old with a moustache; I liked her. "What has happened to you, Beth?" she asked. "You used to be one of my best students, but this year, suddenly your work has gone straight downhill."

I was sorry to make her sad. How to tell her that school and good marks didn't matter any more, all that mattered was music and Paul and where oh where were my breasts? That I was barely awake after the agony of sleepless nights in rollers? That I was doing lots of writing, but poems and my diary, not for her?

"Just really busy, I guess," I said. "I'll try harder, Miss Salton, I promise."

But I knew I wouldn't.

It was hard for me to believe the change in myself. I was still scared of my parents and of the teachers at school, and yet — now there was something else. There was music and true love that made me float.

The Beatles, we heard, had made a movie in England. Soon we'd be able to see them walking and talking, life sized. Unimaginable bliss. All us insane Beatlemaniacs had started going to the Candy

Bowl after school. We'd look through all the fan magazines and shriek, buy packets of Beatles bubble gum and trade the cards, and take crazy pictures of ourselves crammed into the picture machine. This was what real teenagers did.

The next step toward growing up was to tell my mother I wanted to quit piano. "You'll regret this for the rest of your life!" she said. I didn't care. It was my life. Yes, I did like playing when Miss Innis assigned me simple pieces by Johann Sebastian Bach; though I'd never admit it, there was something about that music that felt right in my fingers and in my soul. But I did not want to waste half an hour of my day practicing, or even ten minutes.

My mother was the one who wanted me to go on with piano. She always wanted to play along with me. At the year-end recitals, I'd play a piece or two on my own and then two with her. Miss Innis made a speech about how lucky I was to have such a talented mother to play duets with. Duets! What did Miss Innis know, anyway? Nothing about me, that was for sure.

I'd watched my cracked mother with her cello teacher Ivan, a quiet young musician. The first time he arrived, serious and professional, he showed her the fingering, and Mum, all titters and timid looks, said, "Heavens, Ivan, my fingers just aren't strong enough! How *do* you do it? You'll have to show me again."

Within a few lessons, he too was giggling, blushing a deep quivery red just standing at the front door, holding his cello. That sort of thing happened over and over. My mother couldn't help getting everyone to adore her.

But I fought back. She said the Beatles were a fad that would soon vanish. I had to laugh. To hell with her.

One night, as I sat in my room with a pile of horrible algebra, instead of confiding in my diary, I decided to write a story to keep me company; to keep me warm.

My eyes closed. I was, yes, doing homework right here, at the built-in green wooden desk in my little green room, and Paul was sitting in the white wicker chair right next to me, waiting for me to finish. He was my boyfriend, he loved me, everything I did was important to him. The story just unrolled from my pen with barely a word of correction, as if it had been waiting to come out.

HOMEWORK HELP

"Oh, I can't," I groaned. "I just can't."

Paul looked up from the mag he was reading while waiting for me to finish my homework so we could take a walk.

"What's up? ('Oop' in Liverpuddlian.)

"Homework. Look at it. I'll go nuts," I wailed. He marched over and took me by the shoulders.

"Now, listen. Even dreamy minds like yours 'ave got to do homework." He looked at my books and grimaced. "I'll 'elp."

I shoved my History at him and he gently and patiently went over all the facts and dates, making me repeat them till I knew them by heart. I nearly forgot all my History when I saw him sitting there, so seriously bent over my book, his hair falling into his eyes. And then he'd look up, pretending to be severe and scold when I forgot, or send me into convulsions of laughter imitating the teachers, or sit gazing at me with his dark, velvety, merry eyes.

We began Math. Here he too was weak, and so we learned together. We puzzled through problems, argued through axioms, and decided, through diameters, that it was time for our walk. When we'd returned (he had several smudges of lipstick on his face), we continued the math. He read the problems aloud in his soft voice, then sat back deep in thought. Suddenly he'd do a few complicated things with the ruler, and

looking seriously at me, he'd explain the mass of lines on
the page.
    But his eyes danced — oh, how they laughed!

I could see him, I could feel him with me. The next night, when I tackled math, I pretended Paul was sitting beside my desk, showing me what to do. Such an amiable boy. Unfortunately, no real help with algebra.

After writing a story or poem or in my diary, something inside calmed down, and I could breathe. Just sitting at the desk with a pen in my hand, looking at the letters blooming on the page, the words, my words, the feel of paper under my right hand, then holding a notebook of my own poems and stories — these things were happiness.

෯

THE END OF school was near, and there was a dance coming up. Dances and sock hops at the Halifax Ladies College, the all-girls private school I'd been going to for grades seven, eight and nine, were okay. They'd have been better if I had a boyfriend, but I did not, so a boy would be chosen for me and other dateless girls from the dateless boys at the Halifax Grammar School, Halifax's private boys school. I had a personal connection to that school, not just because my little brother went there — The Halifax Grammar School had been founded in 1958 by my father. He thought the Halifax schools weren't good enough for Dave and wanted to be sure his son got the best education, so he and a fellow parent simply started a school. And yet, amazingly, some of the boys going there were really cute. At the last dance, the date assigned to me, Roger, had not been so cute; his breath smelled, and he talked a lot about his electronics club. I had no idea what electronics were.

But now I was a real teenager. Although going stag was scary, I had great hopes for this dance.

There was as always the tortuous problem of what to wear and how to do my hair. After studying the Eaton's catalogue, Mum and I decided she should make me an elegant blue velvet A-line shift. All the party dresses Mum sewed for me were blue, because blue was her favourite colour and went so well with her blue eyes. The dress had such a scooped neckline that we went to Simpson's Sears lingerie to buy a strapless brassiere, which was stiff and hard so it would stay up by itself. My most grown-up underwear yet. Next I would need a panty girdle rather than just a garter belt to hold up my nylons. I had a figure like a stick, but every girl needed a girdle.

Mum and I fought over shoes, whether I could buy stacked heels, kitten heels, jet heels, Baby Louis heels or squash heels. She won, as she always did, and we bought the lowest ones, squash. Still, they were heels.

The day of the dance, my mother took me to a new hairdresser she'd heard about, whose name was Pierre but who sounded like he came from Newfoundland. He told elephant jokes:

How can you tell there's an elephant in the bathtub?
You can smell the peanuts on its breath.

What's red and white and grey all over?
A can of Cream of Elephant soup.

What a gas! Mum didn't get them, natch. The salon smelled of hair spray and peroxide and was crowded with old women sitting in rollers under the blasting heat of the dryers. Where I ended up too. I'd asked for a flip like Shelley Fabares on the *The Donna Reed Show* and the models in *Seventeen* magazine. But when I

emerged from the giant cone dryer and Pierre took out the rollers
— horrors. The curls stuck straight out from the sides of my head,
like handlebars. He tried to backcomb and hairspray them down,
but it didn't work; as I walked out of the salon, my flip bounced
up and down beside my ears, and I thought I saw Pierre trying
not to laugh. I was trying not to cry. The set cost Mum a lot of
money too — $5! My brother said my head looked like a B-52
about to take off. I said I would strangle him.

I hoped that with my new bra and dress and my sparkling
eyes which I was sure were my greatest beauty asset and my new
Passionfruit Pink lipstick and my mother's Chanel N°5, the boy
wouldn't notice my bouncing hair or all the other hideous things
about me.

When I got to the gym decorated with balloons and paper
flowers, the teachers ridiculous in flowery dresses and corsages,
and was introduced to my date, my heart dropped through the
floor. It could not have been worse. They had paired me with
Andrew Thompson. He was just about the handsomest boy in the
Grammar School, if not in all of Halifax. He was at least fifteen,
suave, sarcastic, cool. His family was rich. And despite all that,
I'd heard he was nice. A boy like Andrew Thompson should have
been with one of the pretty older in-crowd girls. How could they
have made such an embarrassing mistake? For sure, he knew it
too. I wondered if he'd even talk to me.

But he did. He really *was* nice. We found stuff to talk about —
about my going to France and how he'd rather go to a school with
girls. I'd read in *Seventeen* a girl should adopt a boy's hobbies
and always find him interesting, so when Andrew went on about
what kind of sailboat went fastest around Mahone Bay, I tried to
pretend to care.

They played some good music, even some Beatles, and as
we twisted, I told him about my love for them, though not of

course everything. Cute as Andrew was, he was not Paul McCartney.

I was careful not to turn my head too quickly. I didn't want to stab him with my hair.

At the end, "Save the Last Dance for Me" came on, a slow dance. Funny it was that song, the one my mother had bought for me that neither of us liked. Now I liked it a lot. My hands were on Andrew's shoulders; he had one hand on my shoulder and the other on my back, and I felt small and protected. It was special.

At the end, Andrew gave me a friendly hug. When we peeled apart, I realized, to my horror, that the pressure of his chest had squashed the pointy brassiere flat. My blue velvet breasts had completely disappeared.

"Excuse me for a sec," I said, with my arms folded across my chest, and rushed to the bathroom to pop them out again.

He walked me home. When we said goodbye, I didn't know which of us was more relieved.

ON THE LAST day of school, we all brought our autograph albums in to be signed. Everyone had a funny poem or signature. Marilyn signed, "Yours till Niagara Falls." Daphne wrote, "From the queeriest queer you ever will see." I signed mine, "From Beth, an uncurable Beatlemaniac."

Our final exam marks came in. I was sure I'd flunked because of studying so little, especially Current Events, but I'd come second and won a prize, I kid you not. One day I'd get the low marks I deserved, but it hadn't happened yet. Usually I won the English prize, but this year, it was the Scripture prize. Well, the exam was so easy, just telling the interesting Bible stories we'd learned in Scripture class. My dad said he was proud of me, though he also said his friends were teasing him; he was one of the best-known atheists in Halifax, and his daughter had won the Scripture prize.

But he sounded amused.

Though I'd not studied much for exams, I did study, in depth, the Paul Beatle book that had finally arrived, in which he said he liked girls with long hair and fine bone structure. Oh no — not me, on both counts! But then, "She'll most likely have a kind nature, because I don't like mean people." I'm kind, Paul, I told him, and I don't like mean people either.

"We'll have a really fab house with silk wallpaper and fitted carpets, and a swimming pool shaped like a guitar." I wasn't sure what fitted carpets were, and the pool sounded strange — how would you swim in the long narrow bit? But I'd go along with whatever he wanted. That's what a woman did.

"It'll be homely too, though," he went on. "I'll come in from a show, and the fire will be burning in the grate, and my wife will be curled up on the enormous sofa. Maybe there will be two or three little McCartneys upstairs, waiting for me to say goodnight."

Oh yes yes yes. Let me curl up on that big warm sofa right now.

JUNE 18 WAS Paul's twenty-second birthday. He was a Gemini, which meant, according to the Paul book, he was "kind, gentle, sociable, clever, also easily irritated and upset." In other words, a sensitive dreamboat needing a loyal wife to protect him. My fellow Paul Girl Hillary invited me to a sleepover at her house; we listened to *Beatlemania!* and *Twist and Shout* and read *Seventeen* and *Archie* comics and Beatle books, ate angel food cake as Paul's birthday cake and pretended we would send him presents. But although he didn't know it, I'd already given him the best present I possibly could. Me.

As we tried on lipsticks and teased our hair, Hillary's much older cousin Donna pushed through her bedroom door. She had promised to teach Hilly about boys, and I was there at just the right time. Donna was sixteen and had a real boyfriend called Frank. She reclined on Hillary's messy bed, wearing turquoise pedal pushers and a pink sleeveless turtleneck, her dark hair a teased round bubble with a little pink bow at the side, her nails a pointy pink. I envied her grown-up appearance and her boyfriend. Hilly and I perched nearby like dowdy little kids.

"You have to keep one thing in mind, girls," she said, popping a Juicy Fruit into her mouth and offering one to us. "Your job is to play hard to get."

"How do you play hard to get?" Hilly asked, as if she urgently needed to know.

"Frankie knows the rules. First base only, so far. That means necking," said Donna to our baffled faces, "and parking, no petting."

"So what do you do?" Hilly asked, chewing thoughtfully.

"Do?"

"When you and Frankie are necking."

"What do you think we do?" she said, snapping her gum and holding her nails out at a distance for inspection. "We kiss in his car and Frankie tries to touch my boobs, and I let him a little and then push his hands away."

This was enthralling. I wanted to ask her if Frankie was a "biologist" — new slang for "horny wolf," according to the list of teen slang I'd just read in Hillary's *Seventeen* — but I thought Donna might not know the latest cool American lingo. Donna was cool, but she lived in Dartmouth.

My father actually *was* a biologist. That was strange.

"He likes to French kiss," Donna went on. "That's when you touch tongues. Sometimes he puts his tongue in my ear. Makes me feel like I'm on fire."

"Eeeeww!" I said. "I would *never* let a guy stick his tongue into my ear."

Donna laughed. "You say that now, but just wait, sweetie. Lookit." She tilted her head sideways and extended her neck. "And after I told him no."

We gathered around and looked — at her hair? Her necklace?

"It's a hickey! Here." She pointed to a fiery patch that looked painful, like a rash. We gazed respectfully.

"Donna, do boys ever like girls who are flat-chested?" I asked, blushing.

"It's not what you have, Elizabeth, it's what you do with it," she said. "Do you do your exercises every day?" She pushed her forearms up rhythmically. "We must, we must, we must develop our bust. They'll grow. And then you can be Miss Canada. Or at least," she said, flipping through *Seventeen*, "the Clearasil Personality of the Month."

And then Donna and her perfect hair bugged off, taking all her valuable insights with her.

Getting a tongue stuck in your ear, having someone suck on your neck — who could possibly, in a million years, want that?

But next morning, mooning around my room to *Beatlemania!*, my need for Paul hurt my body, my heart. I was one giant throbbing sick-feeling ache.

The way to feel better was to write myself into his life. I picked up my Paul stories notebook and wrote a story about us going steady — sweet, absent-minded Paul pumping up his bicycle tires and taking me to his soccer games and music practices. It ended:

> *Paul was a very popular boy, quietly amusing, masculine and yet not bullying, a good sport and a good friend. Even his dreaminess wasn't held against him — they teased him and then left him alone.*
>
> *But when we were alone, I wasn't a sister or one of the*

guys, I was his girl. As he held me gently in his arms and
kissed me, I knew that, dreamy and enthusiastic or not, Paul
was my life, and I wouldn't complain for the world.

Oh, the power of one little story to whirl me away. I drew and
coloured a picture of the two of us walking into a pink and gold
sunset, arms around each other, with my hair flipped perfectly.
And then scotch-taped on my favourite bubblegum card.
Perfection.

6

July

In July, we had to pack up our house and get it ready for the lucky family who were renting it for the year. Dad said a teenage girl would be in my room so I could leave my Beatle-decorated walls, but the thought of some weirdo in my sanctuary mauling my precious pictures drove me crazy, and I took down a few favourites and hid them in my diary. Dad went through my suitcase and took out everything he said I didn't need, but he didn't touch the pictures, and he even let me bring some Beatle records. He was trying to be kind.

"This is a grand adventure, Bethie," he said, "one you'll never forget."

"Yeah," I thought. "That's what I'm afraid of."

JUST BEFORE OUR departure, we took our beloved dachshund Brunhilda to the Wickenheisers, the German friends who'd given her to us and who'd offered to look after her during our sabbatical. They loved dogs, but still, I held her long sleek body tight and did not want to let her go, my best friend with the silky ears and liquid brown eyes, the only one in the family who listened and understood. What would she think when she turned around and discovered we'd just abandoned her? Would she ever forgive us?

I said farewell to everything else dear — the shelter of my room, the tall dark pines guarding my windows, the wild labyrinth of Point Pleasant Park; goodbye to Frank Cameron, my little pink record player, dear Beatlemaniacs Hilly and Lea. I took a deep breath, gathered all my paper dolls and gave them to Carol's little sister Joanie, next door. *This seems to symbolize giving childhood away, if you know what I mean,* I wrote in my diary. I also wrote a letter to myself, scribbled *To Beth Kaplan when she gets back from France* on the envelope, and hid it in my room. Whoever she was, the stranger coming in, if she harmed any of my things, I'd kill her.

Just before we left town, Hillary gave me instructions: I had to meet Paul over there and persuade him to come live in Halifax, where I could date him most of the time, but she could have him when I was doing other things. I promised, though I knew that was silly. Once he met me, Paul would never want to date anyone else.

WE WERE TO sail on an ocean liner — cheaper than flying — to New York City, where we'd spend a few days visiting family before getting on the big luxury liner to Europe. The night before leaving Halifax, after we'd boarded the SS *Olympia*, a group of Dad's scientist friends came on board for a farewell party in our stateroom. Dad had made a big punch out of fruit juice and lab alcohol, all he could afford, and it must have been really strong because they got loud and nutty. One professor started to say goofy romantic things to my mother; another, weaving his way off the boat, almost fell off the gangplank and a third passed out completely and had to be carried away. Mum was mad about the mess in our stateroom, but Dad didn't care — he was asleep.

The happy family, on its way. Oh brother.

I read *Pride and Prejudice* all the way to New York, when I wasn't throwing up or sitting under a blanket on deck to recover. There were some bits I didn't get, but it was still good. Elizabeth, I thought, is a very fine name. There were a lot of great Elizabeths.

Our second night on board, I started writing one poem, and then another just popped into my head. It amazed me. Where did it come from?

> *Loneliness is a teenager there*
> *Boredom in her eyes, her soul*
> *Cries out for occupation,*
> *Something to achieve, a goal*
>
> *Loneliness is an old man in the park.*
> *His eyes are hollow, sunken, dark*
> *With moody thoughts and hopes*
> *Which never have seen light.*
> *There's nothing he can do. He might*
> *Wander off to some new bench*
> *But in the darkness he still gropes*
> *For reason to live, to wrench*
> *Life from starving heart.*

This one felt like a real poem. I copied it out nicely and gave it to Mum, and she said it was very good. Because of the word "wrench," I thought; that word made it good. I found a way to use it all day. "Giving away my paper dolls," I told her, "was a wrench."

And "starving heart" — also not bad, I had to admit.

❦

LOOMING AHEAD, THERE was New York City, a forest of spikes jabbing the sky. When we went through customs and Dad produced my American passport, I was reminded again of the strange fact that I'd been born in Manhattan but moved to Halifax at the age of three months. On each visit, I thought being born in New York meant I should feel at home there, and I tried to relax and feel I belonged. But I never did. Yet I didn't feel at home in Halifax either.

I was an American from New York, and yet I wasn't. I was and I wasn't a Canadian from Halifax. And also, as our visits to New York always made clear, I was definitely not Jewish. And yet I was.

The whole thing about being Jewish and not Jewish was confusing. Because my mother was Protestant, officially, according to Jewish law, I did not and could not belong to the Jews. But my dad was not really Jewish either, in a way — he was an atheist scientist and disliked all religions. We celebrated Christmas and Easter — at least, the turkey and presents and chocolate eggs part — but except for one Passover with Dad's family on Long Island, we'd never celebrated a religious event on his side.

A few years before, Dad had gone to apply to the Waegwoltic Club, the big Halifax club on the water where almost all my schoolmates spent their summers meeting boys and learning to swim, sail and play tennis. The director of admissions, who was a colleague and friend of Dad's, begged him not to try to join. "It would embarrass the club to have to turn you down," said the friend. Even learned university professors from New York City were not welcome at the Waegwoltic Club, if they were Jews.

And their children were not welcome either, even if their mother was a tall blue-eyed blonde Anglican born in a thatched cottage in an English village. There was a tennis club just down the street that my mother was not allowed to join because she was a Kaplan. All summer long, while my friends swam and sailed at the Waeg, I sat reading books in the garden, on the verandah, in the sharp wind of Lawrencetown Beach.

Once, Hillary invited me to the Waeg as her guest. I spent the day in a miserable stew of feelings: envy, because the place was wonderful, with a clubhouse, tennis courts, swimming pool, sailboats and tons of cute boys in shorts; resentment — why was I not good enough to swim with Christians? — and fear, that an alarm would go off. It would be discovered that a half-Jewish girl was there, and I'd be ordered to leave.

When I told my father about my day, he said, "Fuck 'em if they can't take a joke."

That was Dad's response to a lot of things. On the outside, he was tough, my father — especially in New York. Mum, Dave and I were like timid country mice, but Dad turned into a full-speed-ahead New Yorker the minute we stepped off the boat.

MY AMERICAN GRANDFATHER, Pop, was waiting for us at the docks, as he always was. He was a big, warm man who looked, people said, like President Franklin D. Roosevelt, with little round glasses and one leg that didn't bend, from tuberculosis in his childhood. After hugs, we loaded all our stuff into his giant Buick. In Halifax, my parents drove a bumpy Morris Minor with wooden panels on the back, like a little box. In New York, we floated through the steamy streets in a car like a cabin cruiser, looking at the hot, crazy city from the cool inside.

My grandpa drove us to West 94th where we were staying with my Uncle Edgar, Dad's younger brother, and his wife, Betty. Slow-moving, brilliant Edgar Kaplan was one of the best bridge players in the world, and like Dad, also a musician and a gourmet food and wine lover. He was nearly forty before he moved out of my grandparents' apartment to marry Betty Sheinwold, who'd been the wife of his bridge partner — now his former bridge partner. They lived on the first two floors of their tall, narrow row house, ran *Bridge World* magazine out of the third floor, and the fourth at the top was a little apartment for visiting bridge experts and, occasionally, family. Uncle Edgar didn't like most of his family, but he liked us. Otherwise, he and Betty were only interested in Abyssinian cats, French wine, Johann Sebastian Bach and bridge.

I already knew and liked them, because we visited New York every summer. Dad had a very big family, and though half of them weren't speaking to the other half, all of them were speaking to Dad. He was the favourite. In the course of our stay, it felt as though we had visited most of New York, which meant, besides Edgar and Betty and my grandparents, seeing Belle, Lily, Ben, Vera, Lola, Leo, Sam, Chet, Harry, Hazel, Daniel, Dickie, Debbie, David, Peter, Patti, Teddy, Betsy, Chester, Oscar and Sol. I felt shy and overwhelmed a lot of the time, not just by buildings and speed and noise but by people.

My Kaplan relatives said I looked like my father. At a gathering once, a bony old woman like the witch in *Snow White* seized my arm. "You don't know who I am, darling," she said. "They don't talk about me. I'm Aunt Ann, and you're Gordin's girl. I'd know you anywhere; you look just like your dad."

In England, my mother had almost no family, but we did go to visit her Auntie Edith once. The sweet old lady beamed at me and said, "I'd know you anywhere, dear girl. You are the image of your mama."

Dad was really good-looking, and so was my mother. I was not good-looking, and I looked like them? What, like the not-so-hot side of both my parents? And also, because Dad was Jewish,

I didn't get to belong to the Waeg, and yet because Dad was an atheist, I didn't get to miss school on Jewish holidays.

With my luck, I'd inherited the worst of both worlds.

WE SPENT THE first evening with my grandparents, Nettie and Mike, on West 79th. My little grandma, in her usual shapeless dark blue dress and stumpy shoes, was waiting for us in the hall when the elevator doors opened. Out of the penthouse apartment behind her came the smells of all the food she'd been cooking for days for my dad, all of it hideous. Eggplant. Chicken livers. Purple Russian soup made from beetroots. She thought my shiksa mother was starving us to death.

After dinner — "Eat, darling, *ess, ess, shayna maydel,* you're too thin," Grandma kept saying to me, as I struggled through — there was a slide show. My grandparents had just returned from a grand tour of Europe, and on the eve of our own trip, wanted to show us what was in store. Up on the screen came a picture of my grandma in a dark blue suit, standing in front of a bit of metal. "The Eiffel Tower," said Pop. "My, what a piece of engineering."

The next slide, my grandmother frowning in front of a battered door. "Notre Dame," said Pop. "Awe-inspiring beauty." Next, Grandma beside an edge of bridge. "Venice," chuckled Pop. "No one warned us that the water smelled." The slides went on, with my grandmother blocking out all the landmarks of Europe, until Mum and I turned to each other. Without warning, without being able to stop, we both exploded into laughter.

"What's so funny?" snapped Grandma. "I wasn't aware these pictures were comical."

"I'm sorry, Grandma," I managed to say, mopping my eyes. It was obvious my mother wasn't going to try to fix things, so I had to scramble fast to get us out of this one. "It reminded Mum and me of something funny from back home." I choked back another laugh. But the slide show was over.

It was such a lovely moment, a deep unspoken secret Mum and I shared, like sisters. Too bad my grandparents could not share it too. I felt badly that we'd offended them. But it had been worth it to feel close to my mum.

WE WENT TO the New York World's Fair, where most of all we wanted to see the Futurama. We'd heard so much about this exhibit that showed the spectacular world of the future, with its underwater hotels and farms and an aquacopter to get you there. But we took one look at the mile-long line-up and the sign "Two hour wait" and decided to see other things instead — Spain, Austria, Japan, Mexico, Dinoland and a glimpse, as we rolled by it on a moving sidewalk, of Michelangelo's *Pietà*. Such love and grief in Mary, holding the graceful dead body of her son, all miraculously carved from marble. It was the most beautiful statue I'd ever seen. I hadn't seen many statues, but it was hard to imagine one more beautiful than that.

The next night Pop took us to see *Oliver!* — a terrific musical on Broadway with a very cute star called Davy Jones, who I thought would be fine as a date on the nights that Paul McCartney was busy.

As usual, New York was dazzling — the sparkly crush of Broadway, the mass of skyscrapers and billboards that left almost no sky, the parade of swanky hotels and apartment buildings with doormen and elevators, yellow cabs honking, ambulances blaring, swarms of rushing people and giant cars, blast furnace heat rising from the sidewalk in waves and the smell of gasoline, sweat and spicy food. I'd almost never been in an elevator or a taxi or seen a doorman in Halifax, and I'd been to one musical — *Guys and Dolls* with my school music teacher playing Adelaide, which I adored so much, I'd seen it twice. "That's what I want to do when I grow up," I said to myself, clapping wildly for Miss

Fletcher. "Make an audience happy, like this." In Halifax, it seemed possible to grow up to be an actress and a writer. In New York, I was just a small-town hick.

But also, I wanted to make my American grandparents proud and felt I should be doing more. They were pleased in the days when I was taking lots of classes, and especially when my name was in the newspaper — like reviews of the plays I was in, or when I entered a children's essay competition and won a *Britannica Junior Encyclopedia* set. The topic was to write about your favourite book, so of course I chose *A Little Princess* by Frances Hodgson Burnett. I loved that book so much — the story of Sara Crewe, a kind, imaginative girl who triumphs over cruelty, cold and hunger by making up stories for herself and her friends — that the essay flowed out in five minutes onto a piece of paper spattered with poached egg, and I couldn't believe I'd won. The *Halifax Mail-Star* printed an article with a picture of me holding one of the encyclopedias. My grandfather liked to have clippings in his wallet that he could whip out and show people — Uncle Edgar winning a bridge tournament or my dad doing something controversial, or even, occasionally, me.

But this time, my grandparents were very disappointed that I'd quit piano and everything else. In New York, it was important to do a lot of things and do them well. Better, if possible, than anyone else.

I knew from the stories he'd told that my father had always been expected to be the best. Pop was warm but also critical; he thought Dad wasn't advancing fast enough in his career. "You're too much of a troublemaker, Yankel," he said at dinner, "you use bad language and you drink too much."

Dad laughed. Pop was a very good businessman with his own dress business, Sandra Sage Dresses. This trip, he was going on about miracle products called Dacron and Polly something that he said would revolutionize fabrics. "No ironing, ever," he said. But material made out of plastic did not sound like a great idea to us.

We had a family Chinese banquet, where my father devoured so much food so fast that he took off his shirt so he wouldn't get it dirty and ate in his undershirt. My mother was appalled, but what could she do? Uncle Leo told stories about what a tough, mischievous little boy Dad had been. Mum told me later Dad had to be tough to survive his ghastly mother. I liked my grandma; she was good to me, especially when she took me to the Junior Miss department at B. Altman's and then to Schrafft's for a chocolate soda. But Mum said she was always inventing or exaggerating illnesses, pretending she had a heart condition. Nothing was ever good enough, Mum said, for her two precious sons. One of whom made a disgusting mess swabbing black bean sauce off his undershirt.

ON THE LAST night, Edgar and Betty made a special dinner for us. "Cock o van," Betty told my dad, "from Julia Child. In honour of your travels."

"Vomit," I thought. I'd had it before — chicken drowning in booze.

"Let me at that burgundy," said Dad, heading for the bottles in the dining room.

Close to dinnertime, even I thought the house smelled delicious. We were sitting in their egg yolk yellow breakfast nook off the kitchen, Dad as usual with my brother on his knee. Dave was ten, but he still always sat on Dad's knee. Dad ruffled his curls and teased, "That's my *sonny boychik*," tickling and hugging, Dave giggling, until he slipped off Dad's lap and went upstairs to watch television. I wanted to watch television, but I also wanted to sit with the grown-ups. Betty asked me about France.

"It's scary not knowing what we'll find," I said. "One big black bottomless question mark."

"You'll love it," she said, stirring. "How can you not love Paris?"

"I wish I had a friend there. And I don't know a single word of French except *merci*."

"You'll learn," said my father.

"I would have learned at school in Halifax," I said. "I love my school and my friends and I want to stay home."

My father snorted.

"I understand that, Gordin, for God's sake," said Betty, tasting from a wooden spoon. "I wasn't adventurous at thirteen."

"I don't believe you," said Dad, snuffling in his wine glass. "Beth, go keep an eye on your brother."

"Why?" I asked. "He's fine."

"He doesn't know his way around this house."

"He could find a TV anywhere."

"I didn't ask your opinion. I told you what I want you to do."

"But I want to stay here."

His arm snapped out, his hand up, I was too slow to duck, whack, crack, hard on the side of my head.

"Don't talk back to me," he said. "Do as you're told."

"Gordin, you're a bastard!" shouted Betty. "A bastard."

Eyes swimming, I'd started to get up, but froze — in front of me, a large aluminum pot sailed through the air. From ten feet away in the kitchen, Betty had picked up the chicken dish and hurled it at Dad's head. The entire pot. Dad swerved. The pot crashed against the yellow wall behind him and came clattering down to the floor. Hot chicken sauce splattered all over the walls, the table, Dad, me.

Betty was panting. "Leave that child alone!" she shouted. "It's intolerable. I won't have it."

Everyone breathed in and out. My dad picked up a wad of paper napkins and began wiping his shirt.

"When you have your own children, dear sister-in-law," he said, "feel free to comment on my skills as a parent."

"Your skills as a parent? Are you joking?" she said. "Here, Beth" — she handed me a dish towel — "get cleaned up."

My mother, her face grim, got down on her hands and knees to wipe up the mess.

Uncle Edgar rose in his slow way. "Well, Bear," he said — he and Betty called each other Bear — "you have had your Joan of Arc moment, and now we are bereft of dinner. I'll call Lee Chow."

WHAT JUST HAPPENED? I thought, as I wiped myself off. Had my aunt actually attacked Dad because of me? Me? Was that what she'd meant?

No. No, not possible, there was nothing unusual in what Dad had just done. Then why was she so angry at him? Betty was smart and musical but very eccentric; my parents had said so. She'd always seemed to adore my father.

I SLIPPED OUT of the tense kitchen and vanished upstairs. Maybe I could find New York's Murray the K, the Beatlest DJ, whose show we could sometimes get in Halifax after 9 p.m., when the reception was better. But I didn't dare touch my uncle's complicated radio set. Dave was watching *The Beverly Hillbillies*. What a hilarious show. Especially Jethro and the grandma.

We were called down for a Chinese banquet, all kinds of weird lumpy dishes steaming on the dining-room table. I ate mostly rice. "You will go far," my fortune cookie said. I read it aloud.

"As far as Paris, anyway," said Betty. The grown-ups were joking as if nothing had happened; Betty paid no special attention to me. But when dinner was over, I slipped into the breakfast nook to check. There was a greasy gash in the wall, just behind the chair where Dad had been sitting. It looked permanent.

On the fourth floor, as my brother and I lay in our twin beds, he turned to me. "Why doesn't Daddy like you, Beth?" he said.

What kind of creep would rub it in, that he was the favourite? Then I saw he wasn't being mean. He really wanted the answer.

"I don't know," I said. "He just doesn't." It was the kind of pain that burned.

ONCE I HAD felt as close to my dad as Sara Crewe in *A Little Princess* did to hers. But then something happened. Unlike Sara, I had a brother. When I was nearly four, a baby boy was born into my family, and my father gave his heart away. Dad was so proud of David. Mum said once that after the polio — Dad had polio when I was a baby and nearly died — doctors thought Dad would never walk again, let alone father a son, a ten-pound son at that. So Dave's birth was a big deal. But what was so great about

a big fat son? All Dave had that was special was that thing down there that boys had and I didn't. But that seemed to make all the difference.

Dad had loved me a lot, I was sure of it, when I was little. Somewhere way underneath, so far down I could not say it aloud, I was sure he loved me still. What I needed to figure out was how to change enough to win him back.

THE NEXT MORNING, as I climbed out of bed, my brother pointed at me and crowed, "Your nightgown slipped way down last night and I saw your tits!"

I hated him.

Despite my having to sleep in the same room as my jerky brother, our stay in New York turned out to be wonderful, because I was able to buy the new Beatles LP *A Hard Day's Night*. But there was nowhere to play it. I wished they made little tiny record players you could carry with you and play in secret, so your parents wouldn't hear.

My mother got to go to Tall Girls, which was the only place she could buy her immense size thirteen footwear, and was happy with a pair like little brown canoes. Dave and I were happy because our grandparents bought us clothes, books and magazines. And Dad was just happy because it was New York.

An article in *Calling All Girls* said Paul liked girls who played a musical instrument, and I was angry with myself for quitting piano. As soon as possible, I'd start taking lessons again. Then not only my American grandparents, but Paul, would be pleased.

July 22

I must curl up in a ball, or clench my teeth, or cry or unleash my emotions somehow, when I think of Paul. I have a

71

particular picture, taken on his 21st birthday. George Beatle is holding his legs, Ringo and John Beatle his arms, and they're giving him his "birthday bumps." He is grinning and he looks so helpless and sweet.

Oh, I'm so crazy and I can't express myself. I dream about him — meeting in our childhood, in France, everywhere! The terrible thing about our "love" is that it's so stupidly hopeless, so hopelessly hopeless. There's one zillionth of a chance I'll ever see Paul in life, let alone meet him, waltz with him, date him, love him, kiss him, marry him. So hopeless.

And anyway, there must be at least 500,000 other girls who feel the same way.

And in an article on making out, they advised girls to *keep your physical relationship above his necktie and your string of pearls.* I did not own a string of pearls, so where did that leave me?

Safe. For now.

🍂

IT WAS HARD to admit my father was right, but the *SS France* was fun, a many-levelled playground that smelled of motor oil and salt and that you could not leave. Dave and I spent a lot of time sitting at the soda fountain, playing shuffleboard or splashing in one pool or another. I saw *The Pink Panther* twice, free, in the tiny cinema, and a terrific French movie called *That Man from Rio*, with a sexy star. If French boys were like Jean-Paul Belmondo, I thought, this would be a good year. They were showing an Elvis movie too, but I wasn't interested in him, with his sneer and wiggling hips. At mealtimes, Dad ate like a pig — "Gourmet food and all paid for!" he said, his napkin tucked into his shirt like a kid. "Eat more!" But for once, I was allowed to order what I wanted, chicken or noodles with cheese, so for the whole trip, there were no scenes about vegetables and cleaning my plate.

I read a bunch of books, including *Anne's House of Dreams* by Lucy Maud Montgomery, about Anne of Green Gables and her beau Gilbert after their marriage. Why did even interesting people, like Anne or Jo in *Little Women*, turn boring after they got married? Paul and I wouldn't. And there were cute boys to prowl around watching for too. The tall one with longish hair smiled at me, twice, but we did not talk. It didn't occur to me that we might talk.

The best place onboard was a tiny library no one else ever used, silent except for the boat's loud thrumming. It had thick paper and romantic old-fashioned quill pans with inkwells, so I sat there one rainy day as the boat churned forward, dipping a pen into the ink and scratching carefully across the paper, dabbing sometimes with blotting paper, like Shakespeare. I'd been thinking about Paul's mother, how she died when he was only fourteen, the age I would turn in only a few weeks. What a tragedy that must have been for him.

So I wrote a story about the two of us being best friends back then; we'd meet in a field every Sunday and confide in each other. Then his mother died and was buried on a Sunday. People talked about how brave young Paul was — that he hadn't shed a tear. But after the funeral, he came running to our field, and it was there, holding tightly onto my hand, that he cried.

Finally, his sobs subsided; he was calm again, and even a bit embarassed. I smiled reassuringly, he took a deep breath and let go of my hand. He began to walk off, and I thought, "I'll let him go. He wants to be alone." However, he immediately turned back and asked, "Coming?"

I joined him, he took my hand again in his, and we went together to face the world.

My splashing tears smeared the ink.

When I finished a story or poem, it was stored inside me, tingling, alive. I walked around the decks all that day, feeling Paul's hand in mine. My mother asked why I was smiling.

"Must be the sea air, Mum," I replied. "You were right about that."

I spent as much time as possible in the little library. Just me and Paul and the sea and the ink.

What is it? This sweeping surge
Of emotion, of feeling, the rushing
Like a breaker of the ocean —
Yes, it must be because
Isn't that salt water in my eyes?

❦

OUR TIME IN New York was full of hullabaloo, but in London, there was no noise at all. We sat in the parlour of my British grandparents Marion Edith Alice and Percy Harold Leadbeater, drinking tea and nibbling Granny's cakes and biscuits, and everyone, even my dad at the beginning, spoke nicely and did not interrupt. And especially did not boast. You absolutely must not boast in England, even if you had a lot to boast about, whereas boasting was required in New York, even if you didn't. With my American relatives, I felt too quiet and small; with the British, too loud and big. My English granny wrote to me once that I should stop using so many exclamation marks in my letters. Being an exclamation mark kind of girl was good in New York, not good in London.

Mum told me that during a family visit to England when I was three, Granny had said to her, "You'd better get control over that child right now or she'll be running the show."

I wondered what would be so bad if I did run the show. And what show?

London was different too, because my mother's parents, unlike my dad's, didn't have much money, and we didn't go shopping or to the theatre. I didn't love them less because of that. It was good to have grandparents, even if you didn't know how to be with them. I was no more comfortable with the British ones than with the Americans.

The Leadbeaters were schoolteachers who'd moved during the war from their country village to Barons Court in London, to a ground floor and basement flat that smelled of drains. Only one room was ever warm — the big bright parlour on the main floor, where we had tea, brought up on trays from the damp, smelly kitchen below. My grandparents had only recently acquired a tiny fridge, in which they kept cans — called tins — of peaches and peas and tuna fish, whereas eggs, cheese, milk and butter were kept in a small cupboard in the dining room, called the larder. My grandparents didn't even know how to use a fridge! And they didn't have a toaster — we toasted Granny's home-made bread on a long curly fork in front of the gas fire in the dark basement dining room. It was like going back a hundred years. They did have a small television set, which I instantly wanted to turn on and search for Beatles. No, we had to sit around drinking tea and talking. Quietly.

But the food Granny made was wonderful — plain meat and potatoes and the best dessert I'd ever tasted: a lemon meringue pie made, she said, with four real lemons. When my tongue touched her pie, I understood for the first time that a food besides peanut butter could make you happy. My dignified British granny smelled of lavender and cake. It was hard to like my grandpa, whose hair was stuck flat to his head and who was fussy and humourless, his favourite words, "Oh dear oh dear oh dear." He and my dad didn't seem to like each other much, which wasn't a surprise as they could not have been more different. Dad liked to tell about the time the Leadbeaters were visiting us and, at one dinner, Grandpa snapped, pointing at Dad's wine, "Bottles bottles bottles! That's all you think about — bottles!"

Grandpa didn't like drink. He didn't seem to like children either, or much else, except my mother. He drove a tiny car, even smaller than our Morris. I was nervous driving around London on the wrong side of the road with my tight-lipped grandfather. But it was exciting to see what the cool English kids were wearing, the boys going backward in time — boots with heels, tapered pants and gorgeous long flowing hair like old-fashioned poets, whereas girls were wearing so little, going forward into space age toplessness! I would not be imitating that.

WONDERING ABOUT MY school in France, I lay in bed one night, writing a dreamy story about meeting Paul at the perfect American high school, like the one in the *Archie* comics, where he and I would know right away that we were meant for each other. Just writing a cool story about being with a boy made me feel cooler. Because I was not cool with boys. But when I turned fourteen in a few weeks, I was sure that would change.

HIGH SCHOOL HEAVEN

The moment I saw him, I knew that I must know him, and kiss him. I know that sounds forward and boy-crazy, but that's the sort of boy he was. He had a mop of shining dark-brown hair, which kept falling into his large, dark eyes. His eyes — oh, hypnotism! They were curious, admiring, sweet, black, and huge. He kept smiling at the world-in-general. He was slim and tall — not muscly tough or limpidly feminine, but masculinely strong and gentle, if you know what I mean. The girls were swooning, but I was so determined to get him, like a hunted animal, I didn't even smile when he glanced at me. Oh, those eyes!

"He's Mr. Venus de Milo," I thought. "Mr. Helen of Troy."

NO MATTER WHERE we went in rainy, foggy London — the Victoria and Albert Museum, the National Gallery, Regent's Park — we always arrived back at my grandparents' just in time for tea. In England, it was always time for tea.

The Beatles were probably here, somewhere nearby, having tea too. How could I meet them?

What would I do if I did?

7

End of July

The French people whose apartment we were subletting had left us a list of every single thing in the place, in case we tried to steal their crappy stuff, and on the list was a small, square piece of carpet sample placed over a brown stain on the living-room rug. Daddy read it out loud: "*Un moquette de tapis, beige.* That means 'one carpet sample, beige.' Unbelievable."

When all four of us looked at the carpet sample and began to laugh, I thought, for a moment, "This might just turn out all right."

THE FIRST SURPRISE was that we weren't actually living in Paris. The apartment Dad's friend Jacques had sublet for us was just south of the city in Gentilly, which Jacques, who lived a few floors above with his family, said was a Communist suburb. You couldn't take a regular metro there — you had to get a special suburban train. The building was a giant slab of concrete in a thicket of others just like it. At home, we had a sunny old house with two stories and a big garden. Here it was ten steps, I counted, from the front door to the end of the hall, and our outdoors was a skinny concrete balcony. To the left when you came in was a drippy old kitchen with a fridge that roared like a battleship; to the right a living room with musty furniture and no television set, then a toilet in its own little room, and a bathroom that I thought had another, smaller kind of toilet until Mum explained it was called a *bee-day* and what it was for — which was the most disgusting thing I'd ever heard. Hadn't these people heard of the shower? Or a washcloth?

What mattered most though was that there were three bedrooms. My room had a bed, a desk and a cupboard for clothes, that was it. But it had a door that locked.

My mother complained about the pots and the ancient stove. The beds were creaky, the toilet was medieval and the first night there was a national electricity strike and we ate sardines and bread by candlelight. It was wonderful. Like the shipwrecked Swiss Family Robinson who built rafts and tree houses and figured out how to survive, we were a family in the midst of an adventure that we were living together.

Dad announced that we'd begin sightseeing right away so we could feel the spirit of Paris. How bewildering was that first trip, walking to the metro in Gentilly, the deafening racket and sour smell of the train, changing at Denfert-Rochereau, another ride, long crowded confusing tunnels underground as we changed again, checking the giant maps. Dad explained how to read the maps for the right line. In September I'd be using the metro every day, all by myself, for school.

We got on the clackety elevator and went to the top of the Eiffel Tower. Looking out over the grey roofs of the vast city, I was truly thrilled for the first time — here we were, for real, in the City of Light! Dad pointed out the famous landmarks, Sacré Coeur, the Arc de Triomphe, the Seine, until they were all a blur. We walked down the Champs-Elysées, the widest street you could ever imagine. How beautiful everything was, even ordinary things like door knockers, lampposts and street signs. There were endless rows of tall cream-coloured buildings with black lacy balconies; there were spectacular monuments, some with golden domes, and statues everywhere and ancient churches that Dad luckily wasn't keen on visiting. The mad, honking traffic of tiny cars was like London; the elegantly dressed people, not like London. Mum kept saying, "I feel so shabby, Gord. I must get some better clothes." She kept turning to look at women in their chic outfits. Dad kept reading the menus in front of restaurants and moaning. David looked at toy sailboats and ice creams.

I looked at boys. Not very tall. Hair not long enough. But very cute.

We went to the light and sound show at Notre Dame Cathedral and for a walk in the Bois de Boulogne, which wasn't nearly as nice as Point Pleasant Park, and for a breezy ride right across Paris standing outside on the open back of an old-fashioned bus. Dad said these buses were being phased out and soon we wouldn't be able to ride out there any longer. He wouldn't stop speaking his fluent French, scraping the r's out of the back of his throat in that annoying way, but at first we were glad, because otherwise we couldn't have gone anywhere. The rest of us just said *merci, bonjour* and *s'il vous plaît*. When I got hungry, I learned my first new word: *sondweech*. Dad said that even though he was longing to eat in restaurants, we didn't have enough money.

"We're on half salary for the whole year, kids," he said, slapping his thin wallet, "and we really can't afford to be here at all." So we went home to eat, stopping at the local stores to buy bread and paté. I didn't know what that brown stuff was made of, but smeared on thick pieces of crusty white bread, the *sondweech* tasted pretty great.

We went to the Louvre. Dad had warned us it was big, but big didn't even begin to describe it – a monster museum, crammed with culture. Though Mum loved it, she said it gave her brain indigestion. We trailed through one immense room after another, looking at a million paintings, some even I recognized — giant canvases of people drowning or having arrows shot into them, many embarrassing naked men and women, thousands of pictures of Jesus's mother and portraits of people who were now dead. And the most famous face of all, the *Mona Lisa*. After looking for a while, I thought, well yes, she's mysterious and beautiful and all that, but I didn't get why she was the most famous face in the world when there were so many other beautiful faces on the walls all around her.

After the *Mona Lisa*, we saw the *Winged Victory* and the *Venus de Milo*, who had a nose with no nose bridge just like my neighbour Carol's — the three Paris works of art I'd learned about in school, and now I'd seen them in the flesh, so to speak. I couldn't wait to write home to tell my school friends that Mrs. Ryan's art appreciation class had come to life; that famous art wasn't just pictures in a book. As we stood looking at smooth white Venus with a face so real you wanted to talk to her, an American tourist in madras Bermuda shorts beside me said, "Where's her arms? Why didn't the artist find a model with arms?"

I tried not to sneer. But I had studied the *Venus de Milo*, and I was not a tourist. I lived here.

My Paul lived here too. Day and night, we shared my sparse room in Gentilly. I had lots of time and not one friend to talk to. So I talked to him.

Time for me to invent a beautiful rosy Paul dream, I wrote in my diary, *so my head will be up in the clouds and I can leave earthy unpleasantness behind. I'll manage to think of something and go over and over it, like a cow chewing her cud.*

One night, Paul and I met at a dance neither of us had wanted to attend. He suggested we get away from the noise and go outside for a walk. And we fell in love, in love, in love. Oh the warmth of his body against mine.

The last line went, *I felt as if a beautiful bubble had encased us, and the slightest noise would break it, like an eggshell.*

Like an eggshell. God, I loved that. I was inside that bubble with my sweet boyfriend, and nothing would wrench me out.

But on a bad day, alone as always in my room, I drew a picture, a self-portrait. It was hideous. There were many days when I loathed myself. What to do about those horrible days, I wasn't sure, except to hope they would pass.

It was always there underneath, the belief that I was too ugly and unpleasant to love. Sometimes I thought myself the least desirable creature ever born. And I'd remember my encounter, two years before, with Lucky.

Carol was dating a pimply boy called Jimmy. I was in her room one day waiting for her to get off the phone and looking at her collection of pink lipsticks from Zellers — though she wore only white lipstick these days — when she told me Jimmy's friend Lucky was over at Jimmy's and wanted to talk to me.

"To me?" I asked. "As a joke?"

"He won't bite," she said. "You have to start sometime."

I took the phone, a pink Princess phone that I coveted. "Hi, Lucky," I said, my voice only shaking a little. "How you doin'?"

After our time in London, I still had a bit of an English accent, and kids said it made me sound stuck up. I did my best not to.

"Great," said a deep voice. "You Elizabeth from next door?" And we talked. Just like that, I was talking to a boy, older too, he fourteen and I twelve. Every time I went to Carol's, she'd be talking to Jimmy, and if Lucky was there, we'd talk too. Since he was not actually in the room, I wasn't nervous and could goof around and make him laugh.

"Yeah, Carol's right here," I said, "but I can hardly see her under her tower of hair."

Carol told me Lucky wanted to see and maybe meet me. We'd go strolling down our street, and the boys would walk past us going the other way. This was real. I felt sick. Carol wanted me to tease my hair, put on her lipstick, eye shadow, eyeliner and tight clothes. But I couldn't. He'd already heard a voice over the phone that wasn't me. If he saw someone who wasn't me either, what was the point?

So Carol and I went out for the walk. It was, worse luck, a drizzly day in Halifax; the foghorn was moaning, and my hair, already flat, got flatter. I had on my khaki suedette car coat, comfortable and "me," but the farthest thing from sexy. There they were in the distance, Jimmy taller, both with hair slicked back, Lucky's with a long swoop over his forehead, like Troy Donahue. They were both really cute. They were terrifying. They drew close.

"Hi," said Jimmy.

"Hi," said Carol.

I said nothing, just kind of looked down in an interesting, thoughtful way, and Lucky didn't say anything either. I was breathless, praying he'd like me. He and Jimmy walked past. And then I heard what Lucky said. He said, *"That's* Elizabeth?"

The things that stay with you are usually not the nice things. Lucky's voice stayed with me. It told me boys didn't like girls who could not be bothered to fix themselves up. And who didn't have big breasts. Or indeed, any breasts.

MY BIRTHDAY WAS coming up in a few days, a very special one: August 1, 1964, was the day I'd turn fourteen. Thirteen had been an important birthday, because it meant becoming a teenager, but fourteen felt much bigger. When I was small, one of the neighbour girls, Andrea, was fourteen. Andrea was just right, with a wide white smile and shiny hair that swung around her face. Year after year, as my birthdays went by, I longed for the fourteenth, because that's when I'd be like her. At eleven, twelve and thirteen, however, it was clear that achieving Andrea-ness would take some doing. But there was hope.

I wondered what my parents had planned for my very special birthday.

After we'd unpacked and bought some supplies, and I'd pinned up my Beatles pictures and was feeling more settled, Dad proposed that we all make an excursion down Boulevard St.-Michel, near the Sorbonne University where the students were. Now this was really gear — crowds of young people. I devoured the way they were dressed, the girls in light summer dresses and matching sandals, so elegant, their hair perfectly styled, flipped up or under but not overdone. I envied their ease and style, their little neckerchiefs, their cigarettes.

We stopped in a shop called Gibert, which Dad said was a famous bookstore, where he bought me a new journal, a French one with a green plastic cover and little squares on the pages instead of lines. I wanted to rush home and start writing in my new green notebook. But I wanted even more to stay on this exciting Boulevard St.-Michel. Maybe eat a sondweech with some paté.

"Pupikina," he said as we stepped outside into the bright July sun, "you need some help getting your French up to scratch before you start school. So I've had a good idea."

Another good idea. My stomach went cold. My mother looked apologetic.

"My Belgian friend Pierre has a lovely daughter, Martine, just a little older. You met her once not that long ago, though perhaps you don't remember. In a few days, she's going on a hiking and camping trip in the mountains of France with her Girl Guide troupe. And I've arranged for you to go with them."

I wanted to throw up on his sandals.

"Martine and the girls are very nice," he went on, "and that kind of immersion is the best possible thing for your French."

I looked at my mother of the zero spine. Surely she would not allow this catastrophic thing to be forced on me. She did not speak.

We had gone on camping trips as a family, and I'd hated every second. Just seeing a picture of a spider made me scream. If God wanted us to sleep on the damp hard ground with spiders, why did he invent comfy bugless bedrooms? As for hiking, nothing appealed to me less than marching vigorously about for no reason. This was the worst thing they had ever done to me. Well, Dad had done, and Mum had gone along with, like always. Nothing I said, no amount of tears or begging, would change his mind.

What made it worse was that that the departure date was August 1, my birthday, when I was supposed to turn into sweet, shiny Andrea. Instead, the day before, my hair was cut short for the trip, my face was blotchy from crying and I was shopping for camping equipment with my parents. Not the dainty summer dress and white sandals with a kitten heel I'd dreamed of — no, hideous bulky brown shorts and hiking boots. Not the white handbag with a gold chain all the girls at home would be desperate to own but a giant orange hump to strap on my back. My nails and cuticles were bitten down so low, they bled. I prayed for an earthquake in Paris, or Belgium, or both.

At night, I filled in the first page of my new journal. It was important to define just who I was, what was important and what was not. So I worked hard at making a list.

FRANCE DIARY JOURNAL

PRIVATE.

NAME: Elizabeth Kaplan.
NICKNAME: Beth
AGE: 13 years
HEIGHT: 5'5"
EYES: hazel
HAIR: medium brown

*LIKES (brief): Paul McCartney, shopping with the intention
of buying, being "in" in a group, laughing, jewelery, reading,
dachshunds, chocolate, fires (in fireplaces), T.V., looking sexy,
English boys, being popular, ballet, money, gentle people,
horses, beautiful things, tapered trousers, parties, dreaming,
movies, writing, black socks for men, high boots for women,*

*HATES (brief): unnecessary noise, going to the dentist, Latin,
crying children, going to bed early, my parents when they are
unfair or angry, the Dave Clark Five, intolerance, freckles,
movies which are bloody and gorey, most vegetables, school,
my nose, being left out, pimples, lonliness, sleeping in bristle
rollers, cruelty, women with hairy underarms, snobs, disor-
ganization, uncivilized camping, women with painted faces,
breath that smells, chainsmokers, exaggeration, going to a
new school, phonies, people who don't answer my letters, being
bored, show-offs, being contradicted, detours, hurrying, school
(again), getting up early, bossiness, aimless hums, rules and
regulations, boredom*

After reading about Paul's supposed girlfriend and her family,
I added:

*Jane Asher, a disgusting horrible rat; Peter Asher her brother,
a finky creep who sings the songs the Beatles write for him;
bullfighting*

The morning of my birthday, I lay in bed for as long as
possible in my shabby room, pretending to be somewhere else —
on the boat home, for example, or hiding somewhere in the
world, in a luxury hotel with Paul. When I got to the kitchen, my
parents were all hearty cheer and produced an Agatha Christie, a

Georgette Heyer and some spending money for the trip. Dad tried to hug me, and I went stiff. Did he really think he could buy my forgiveness with ten francs and two novels? I went into my room, locked the door and wrote dark things in my green plastic diary.

Then it was time to put on my new blue Guide uniform and head off. For an added bit of joy, my period had just started, only the third time I'd ever had it, and I had cramps. I was numb with dread. Dad borrowed Jacques' car to drive to the fanciest train station on earth. And there they were, twenty-seven hearty girls in blue, marching toward us in their boots, with orange humps, just like mine, strapped to their backs. I despised every single one of them, but not as much as I despised my parents.

Dad gabbled in French to one, who smiled at me, shook my hand, said "Théa," and called over a blonde girl, Martine, whom I remembered vaguely and who also smiled and shook my hand. And then they all turned toward the train, Théa gesturing for me to follow. Struggling to control my face, I hugged and kissed my mother, who said, "They're a marvellous group, Beth. It'll be such fun."

I turned and walked off. I would never hug my father again as long as I lived.

Someone helped me swing my pack onto the train and find a seat, and we began to speed away from Paris. The girls were looking at me kindly, but soon they began to settle in for the long ride, reading big comic books, opening packs of cookies. Martine was sturdy with thick hair and wide red cheeks. She tried to talk and laugh, making gestures and faces — yes, no, you, me. We'd be sitting in our seats all night, that much was clear. Some girls were actually falling asleep. I had trouble sleeping in my own bed on a still Halifax night.

Perhaps it won't be too bad, I thought, looking out the black window at my white face floating there, like a ghost looking back. We'd be lodged in a youth hostel perhaps, or a small hotel. I could get away from them — find a radio, listen to the hit parade, hear some Beatles; stroll around town and go shopping with my birthday money. For white sandals, say, and teen magazines. You'll be fine, I told myself; only thirteen days and it'll be over. Only thirteen days with a pack of strangers in the middle of nowhere, doing things I hated doing in a language I could not speak. What could be better?

Tears ran down my cheeks and into my mouth, but luckily there was no one to see. The narrow train screeched through the night, and all around me, girls leaned on each other and slept.

At lunchtime the next day, we arrived wherever it was we were going. The sun shone on a pleasant small town with snow-capped mountains all around. My heart lifted. I heaved my pack into a waiting truck with the others. And then we began to hike — through the town, out of the town, into the country. We walked through a wood and along a dirt road. I was hungry and thirsty; my feet hurt, my back hurt, my eyes hurt from not crying. Where were we?

We were in a field surrounded by mountains. Théa gestured blissfully and gabbled. Thank God, we got to sit in a circle on the ground and were given bread, cheese and warm juice. Théa and her fellow counsellors opened the big duffel bags they'd been carrying slung between them, and I saw tent poles. Tents. We were going to live in the middle of this field, in the middle of France, in tents.

Martine showed me how to set up my bed and my stuff in a tent with her and four other girls, and then we had time to ourselves. One girl got out a guitar, and the others began to gather. Great, I thought, a Belgian hootenanny, how's that for fun, and headed to a river that cut through the bottom of the field. Perching on a big rock just beyond the spray, I clutched my new green notebook to my chest and watched the French river flow by. From there, no one could hear me cry. But I sure could hear them sing.

I wrote to my parents.

> *Well, here I am, it's Monday the 3rd, and I'm miserable.*
> *I'm very sorry — I know you wanted me to like it, I have more than a week left to decide, but at this time, I'm miserable. (I can hear Daddy sneering.) When I'm homesick and can hardly keep back a torrent, I keep saying to myself, "How lucky you are to be here. Look at the lovely scenery. Think of those miserable people in Nova Scotia, and here's you in France with nice Scouts." But it does no good.*
> <u>*Mum, I have never missed you so much in my whole life*</u>*. You know, if there is such a person, perhaps God saw how our relationship was deteriorating and seperated us. I have made a resolution to try not to provoke my family.*

I promised my mother we'd get along from now on, that I'd be good. Maybe this hellish trip was punishment for being so rebellious.

OVER THE THIRTEEN days, the crying stopped; I figured out how to survive. The important words were *pah*, bread, *lo*, water, *fah*, hungry, and *lee*, bed. And *non merci*, I was good at that. Though I couldn't talk to anyone, since none of them spoke English and I spoke no French, it was clear the Guides were nice girls, Théa especially, and Martine was wonderful. I appreciated that, like my mother, she had some kind of heart condition and so would beg off hiking sometimes. Théa reluctantly let her stay behind, and I, with my usual unselfish thoughtfulness, offered to stay with her. We'd lie in the grass and talk as best we could with a few words of French and English and our hands. She loved the Beatles too.

"Je (goobledygook) George," she said, pointing to her heart.

"George?!" I exclaimed. He was nice but so quiet, how could any girl choose him? "Moi (pointing to heart) Paul. Paul (pointing to heart) moi."

We laughed. This was way better than puffing up a mountain with Théa pointing at cloud formations and moss. I was grateful for Martine. The days passed, and I was still alive.

As often as allowed, I sat on my rock by the river to watch the foam and still, sometimes, cry. I kept remembering how delicious Mum's baking was, how she cooked nutritious meals, even if, most of the time, I didn't like what she made. Best of all, when I was sick, she'd bring flat ginger ale and lay a cool hand on my hot forehead; as soon as I started to feel better, she'd make her homemade macaroni and cheese. When Mum appeared by my bed carrying a tray with a plate of creamy macaroni, a cup of tea and fresh flowers in a little pot she'd made in her pottery class, it meant for sure this bout of measles, chicken pox, mumps, tonsillitis or flu was over.

How it pained me to remember that tray, sitting by the river.

I THOUGHT A lot about my parents, how they could be okay one minute and loathsome the next. My mother, who wanted me to be her best friend or her sister. She wanted me to tell her my secrets, so she could tell me her secrets. Mum had lots of secrets — about Dad, about her past — and I wasn't sure I wanted to hear them.

And my father, the architect of so much misery, who never paid the slightest attention to what I said or thought.

"Parents should do whatever they feel like with their kids," Dad liked to say, "because whatever they do, it will be wrong."

This was not a helpful philosophy. He and my mother were interesting people and had good points, even I could see that. They weren't hopeless as people. Just as parents.

I had to wonder, sometimes, if the two of them even loved each other. There were times when they were cuddling and smooching enough to make you sick, and other times when they did not seem to even like one another at all. Mum would get up in the middle of the night to write Dad long letters about what he was doing wrong that made her unhappy. Then things might be better for a few days, though sometimes nothing changed. Dad did not change.

Lots of people were crazy about my dad, and the most confusing thing was that sometimes I was crazy about him too. My generous, funny father and I laughed at the same things, like the jokes my mother never got but that I always did. Like the one Dad liked to tell about the guy whose penis got shot off and was replaced with the trunk of an elephant. He said it worked just like the old one, "except," he said, "when someone passes me with a plate of peanuts."

So funny.

Dad was handsome, tall and vigorous with eyes the exact same greeney brown as mine. People said that with his thick dark hair and boyish grin, he looked like John F. Kennedy. Besides his work as a scientist and professor, he was passionately involved in his causes, spending a lot of time volunteering and raising money for the March of Dimes to help people crippled by polio, as he himself had nearly been. And he cared madly about world peace. For years, he'd been leading a big national campaign against the dumping of radioactive nuclear fallout in Nova Scotian waters, with appearances on TV and radio and speeches across the country. Several of his long articles about Strontium 90 and the dangers of nuclear proliferation had been published in *Weekend* magazine, with pictures of "Dr. Kaplan's family," which was us. I tried to read what he was saying but couldn't get past the second line. He had his own local television show for a while too, *Crossfire*, debating controversial issues with guests, though unless he rented a TV set, we couldn't watch it. I must have been the only kid in Halifax who knew what Strontium 90 and nuclear proliferation were, and why they were bad.

Dad knew all about history, geography, classical music and science, but he couldn't explain the simplest thing to anyone without a Ph.D. He knew just about everything, except how to listen to young people and music written after the Middle Ages. But still, he was working hard to save the world. Who wouldn't admire that? My friends did; they all really liked him, especially my crazy friend Hillary, who adored him. And he, her.

But lots of people in Halifax did not like my noisy, aggressive father. And now, almost all the time, that included me. It made me sad to think it, but it was true. Though right then, I would have given anything to hear his voice.

I WAS SO lonely, I even reminisced about my brother. At the kitchen table once doing homework, I wanted some milk and asked David to hand me a glass. He picked up a glass, put it to his bum, farted into it and passed it to me.

Honestly. Who could love someone like that?

I wished Dave and I could be friends. He was the only brother I'd ever have; we had to go through so many things side by side. If he weren't there, I'd be an only child, and that would be sad. But I couldn't help it. He'd stolen my father. I hated him.

And I thought about myself. How there was something wrong with me. A girl who boasted, showed off, wanted to be noticed, and yet really didn't. Born into the wrong family. I was an alien, some weird intruder my family had to put up with.

And yet I missed them all so much, as I sat in my spot by the river, I thought I would dissolve.

WHAT KEPT ME company, what kept me sane, was love. Sitting on my rock, damp with mist, I dreamed Paul and I were here in the French Alps together, zipping about on our matching Hondas, mine pale blue and his dark grey. And then I scribbled stories about our true, true love.

> *We sat there in the darkness, his strong arm encircling*
> *my shoulders, loose but sweetly heavy. He drew me closer*
> *and I put my head on his shoulder. He fondled my hair.*
> *I raised my head and we looked at each other, searching*
> *hungrily in each other's eyes. We found what we wanted.*
> *He drew me into his arms and — oh, breathlessness and*
> *electric shocks — gave me a long, thrilling kiss. I whispered,*
> *"Oh, Paul."*
>
> *… Next morning, he called for me and we ran, hand in*
> *hand, to school. I felt I would burst with happiness. But that*
> *evening, as we sat on a park-bench, I asked him if he was*
> *serious. I explained that I loved him and did not ever intend*
> *to be coy or play hard to get.*
>
> *And I still remember how soft and sweet was his voice,*
> *and what a burst of love I felt when he replied.*
>
> *"That," he whispered, brushing my hair from my eyes,*
> *"is why I love you."*

Imagining that moment gave me a physical pain inside. Everywhere.

My whole time with the Guides, Paul stayed by my side. But reality hit me too, and I couldn't help but feel discouraged. *How stupid you are,* I wrote in my diary. *You'll never get within 600 miles of Paul. And if you did, you're just a face in the crowd. And if you weren't, he's* seven years older. *You're too young.*

Actually, I calculated later, he was eight years and one and a half months older. Even worse.

At home, I drank my tea unsweetened, just a bit of milk. With the Guides, I started to take my tea with three lumps of sugar, not just because I was hungry all the time — though the Guides ate at such strange hours (breakfast mid-morning, lunch mid-afternoon and supper in the middle of the night) that I *was* hungry all the time. But Paul, I'd read, took three lumps of sugar in his tea.

The trouble with your romance, I wrote, as I'd written before, *is that it's shared by 600,000 other girls who've also never seen him.*

ON OUR SECOND last evening, we marched off toward the town. *Restaurant,* they told me, a word I understood perfectly. As usual, I was starving and had a fantasy of ordering a huge dish of macaroni and cheese. Oh, for nice plain macaroni and cheese.

We got cheese, all right — a local speciality called *fondoo,* a big pot of melted stinky cheese in the centre of the table, with sticks and big baskets of bread. You stabbed the bread with the stick and dunked it in the cheese, which had long gooey yellow strings that trailed up as you stuck it in your mouth and groaned with pleasure. At least, they did, the Guides. I wouldn't touch it, not with a smell like that, though they kept begging me to try. I ate bread, chewy and white and good.

What was unbelievable was that in the restaurant in this town — Vallouise, population about two hundred — there was a jukebox. And on that jukebox, guess what? "I Want to Hold Your Hand." So gear. I put it on and jiggled in my seat, singing along, while they ate their *fondoo.* I could tell most of the girls liked it. There were some secret Beatlemaniac hearts under those frumpy blue uniforms.

I'm grateful to the Guides, who are really sweet, I wrote in my diary. *But I like cities and civilization better.*

THE LAST NIGHT, Théa made it clear the new girls were going to go through some sort of test. We were summoned to the fire, one by one. They helped me understand: I had to do various foolish tasks, the last one to sing a Beatle song. There in the French Alps, in front of twenty-seven Belgian Girl Guides with a bonfire snapping behind me, I belted out "She Loves You," playing a left-handed bass guitar, bouncing up and down and waggling my head like Paul on *Ed Sullivan*. They all clapped in time and gave me a round of applause. It was the most fun of the whole godforsaken trip.

The new girls were given a new name and an adjective. My name was César — Caesar. The Roman leader, I thought — wow, they really think I have potential. But no, Théa explained slowly, smiling. In the French version of the Walt Disney movie *Lady and the Tramp*, the bloodhound with the long, droopy face and big, mournful eyes was named César.

Very funny.

My adjective was — Théa spelled it for me — *pressée*. Hurried, they translated, speedy. They imitated me — always in a hurry, rushing to be somewhere else. Never happy to be just there, right where I was.

I sure was *pressée*. To get out of that damn tent and into my own *lee*.

8

August

After thirteen days lying under canvas, I thought our shabby apartment in Gentilly looked like a palace, Paul smiling on my walls, the shining toilet with a seat, people speaking English. Food at the right time. Dad told me Théa had telephoned to say she was sorry "Beth did not enter into the spirit of the trip." Perhaps, she'd suggested, I could try again when I was older. Not on your life, I thought. But Dad wasn't mad; he chuckled. I decided not to keep up the silent treatment with him. It would just be too hard.

Mum said she'd missed me, and I told her about sitting by the river and Martine and César. She was very sympathetic, gazing at me with her soft blue eyes. "I knew the trip would be too much for you, darling," she said, "but your father insisted. And I'm sure it was good for your French."

That night when she and I were doing the dishes, I decided to confide in her. Normally, I would have phoned Lea or Hillary. Here — no friends, no choice. She didn't have any friends here either.

"Mum," I said, "what do you think it would be like, being married to Paul McCartney?"

"Absolute hell, I should think," she replied, handing me a saucepan. "He's too well known."

"That's a point," I said, "but we'd overcome it by moving to Afghanistan or something." The remotest place on earth.

"The fact that his mother died when he was young is good," she said, "because men without mothers learn to take care of themselves."

"Holy moly. I never thought of that."

"But he's too good-looking, Beth. Men like that are dangerous. He knows that as soon as he bats his eyelashes, women will come running."

"But he'd be so infatuated with me," I protested, "he wouldn't even notice anybody else!"

My mother smiled a sour little smile. And that was as far as we got, for she began telling me about the latest fight between her and Dad. How they disagreed on money and raising us and everything else.

"We just weren't meant for each other," she said, fishing for her Kleenex. "He's so demanding! I'm desperate."

What could I say? Gosh, Mum, if my dad is so awful, go get a divorce ha ha? I tried to absorb it all without replying and escaped to my room as soon as possible. She'd have to take care of her own problems — I had too many of my own. Dad was crabbier than ever here, maybe because we had no money and were squashed together all the time, and Mum and David were even more annoying. As I'd predicted, there was no way to get away from them. I had never felt so friendless.

Except for my diary. My diary was my best friend. I marvelled that almost none of my schoolmates at home kept one. How could people just live through their days, doing, experiencing and not *noting*? I stuck pictures in the green notebook too: a photo of the river in the mountains that had been my comfort for thirteen days; pictures of Paul. I wrote about my family's daily experiences, but also every single thing I was feeling, especially when things were bad.

Once again, I felt close to Anne Frank. My diary wasn't anywhere near as good as hers, for sure. But this wasn't a competition between us. We were two girls in the same line of work.

Sept. 4

I thought once we arrived in Dad's dream city, Paris, he would be happy and perhaps our relationship would improve. Well! One minute he's love, hugs and kisses, the next, he's snapping, snarling and hitting. He hates me, I'm sure. I'm a robot to be pushed around and slapped when it pleases you to slap.

I must be kind, cheerful, diligent, smiling etc. while he's around. Which I cannot. Perhaps compare me to Ringo. Moody.

September 5

Sometimes when I'm really desperate and feel near tears, I say to myself, "Courage, you idiot. Imagine if Paul walked in now and saw you snivelling." It has been a great help.

But I have my worries and doubts. Is Paul only skin-deep handsomeness? He's not religious at all. Is he phony? Conceited? Affeminate? My heart screams "no" but my mind considers carefully.

"After all, Beth," it says, "he must be losing some of his appeal for you. Three months ago he had no faults at all!"

☙

IT WAS STILL a few weeks before school started, and my parents were busy with maps. The plan, I was informed, was for us to pile into Dad's new dark blue Peugeot station wagon and travel through France to Germany, then to Switzerland and back. Camping, of course. Just what every teenager cherishes, the chance to sleep between her snoring parents and her fiend of a brother in an orange tent made for midgets.

When we got to the German border, both my parents were distressed. In 1946, Mum had worked in refugee camps in northern Germany with Jewish and other victims of the war. Dad, who'd been in an American army MASH unit in France, had tended some of the Jews who'd survived the concentration camps. "I'm a pacifist," he said, "but there was never a more important war for a Jew to fight than that one."

For them both, it was their first time hearing German since those days, except for when we visited our good friends the Wickenheisers in Halifax. When Rudi Wickenheiser was hired as a biologist at Dalhousie, Dad discovered that he had been in the German air force and had dropped bombs near Dad's US army medical unit in France. And now our families were the best of friends; they gave us our adorable sausage dog, and for this leg of our journey they'd arranged for us to stay with Rudi's parents in the Black Forest. Not two decades after the end of the war, a man who'd flown bombers in the Luftwaffe was good friends with the most outspoken Jew in Halifax.

And I'd arrived in Germany with a copy of *The Diary of Anne Frank* in my purse.

At the border, the guard came over to our window and spoke a stream of German to my father, who responded in his own inventive mix of Yiddish and English and handed over our passports. The guard bent over to check on us through the windows, stamped our passports and waved us on. He even smiled.

Dad drove a bit further, pulled over and stopped. He was pale, breathing hard.

"Just hearing that language curdles my blood," he said.

"Dreadful," said my mother.

We knew, as we drove into the small Black Forest town, that Rudi's father had been a member of the Nazi party. And here, to stay with them for a few days, was an entire family named Kaplan.

THE ELDERLY COUPLE lived in an old-fashioned wooden house tucked into a hillside. They welcomed us with open arms — hugs all round. Rudi Senior, a doctor, had thick white hair, a ruddy face and beaming eyes; his wife was big and round, her hair in a neat bun, her cheeks leathery from gardening and long walks. They fed us a huge supper, and next morning an even bigger breakfast with eggs, meat, fresh bread and delicious homemade jams. We slept in rustic wooden beds, not under sheets and blankets but under puffy warm eiderdowns — the first time I'd pulled one over myself. They wore strange sandals too, with one strap across the top and a cloppy wooden sole. Our German friends at home also wore them, but I'd never seen them on anyone else.

The Wickenheisers did not speak English; my mother, who'd learned German doing her refugee work, did much of the translating, but Dad just let loose with his own mix. "*Gib mir a shtickl brot und a bissel schlag, bitte*," he said in Yiddish mixed with German, to receive a dollop of whipped cream on his toast.

Still, I could see that beneath his exclamations of delight at the hospitality, Dad was uneasy. This house might have flown a Nazi flag. Though Rudi had never discussed it, his parents must have known what Hitler was doing to their Jewish neighbours. What had they thought? Their mountain town was so quaint,

I expected Heidi to come skipping along with her goats. Yet as we meandered around, I quivered with outrage at my friend Anne's terrible death — here, in this country, at the hands of these nice Christian people.

And yet, the Wickenheisers were so kind, their jam so fruity on warm sweet buns after a night burrowed into a nest of down. As Dad blundered around, the people we met were friendly and helpful. *It's a beautiful country*, I wrote in my diary. *Prosperous, clean and jolly. Of course, I can't say how things are in the north or on the other side of the wall. The wall — that sounds so ridiculous, like a garden fence.*

When our time was up, after a grateful goodbye to our hosts, I left bewildered. What did these hospitable Germans have to do with mass murder? Nothing, surely. Still, only twenty years ago, right here in this tranquil place, innocent people had been rounded up and shipped away to die.

In all the places we went in Germany, there were reminders of the war — disabled and blind people, destroyed sections of towns and cities. *All because a maniac wanted power!* I wrote. *How lucky Canada was. How much my country missed.*

There were plaques all over Paris too, all over Europe, memorials where people had been killed during the Second World War — and the First World War. I was grateful to be Canadian, and young.

WE CAMPED AND sightsaw and drove. The greatest thrill of the drive back was stopping in a Swiss town called Bienne. It was raining so we went to a local tearoom for supper, where I was ecstatic to discover Beatle songs on the jukebox. Also one they'd titled "The Hyppi Hyppi Shake." I had enough money to listen to a few, and when I put on the exquisite "Things We Said Today," Dad said, "Now that's the kind of rock 'n' roll I like, not those Beatles which isn't even music."

What a fine moment when I turned to him and said, "That IS the Beatles. And their own composition too." Victory!

I also put on "Pretty Woman" by Roy Orbison. Dad made fun of it. I'd heard and loved it before and tried to love it here, but as sometimes happened, listening through my father's ears took away a lot of my pleasure. Maybe it wasn't such a good song after all.

We were all in a great mood over dinner. Hot dogs were the cheapest item on the menu, so Dad ordered four.

"How many pairs do you want?" asked the waitress.

"Pairs?" said Dad. "I'm not ordering shoes, you know." It turned out their hot dogs came attached together. We were giddy with laughter.

In Lausanne, we saw an exposition about nuclear disarmament. At places like that, I felt shallow, ashamed I didn't think more about world events. And yet, *I think I'll wait until I'm older before I worry deeply over the fate of mankind*, I wrote. *I'm too involved with myself at the moment.*

By the next evening, in Geneva, we had almost no money left, and it was raining. Luckily, a Swiss scientist called Kraft, a Dalhousie colleague of Dad's, was there visiting his mother and had invited us to say hello. We prayed they'd ask us to stay, even to camp on their floor. The mother lived in a beautiful apartment in a hotel, and they took us to dinner at a nearby restaurant, which Kraft paid for — it cost $12!

"Shall I book you a room in our hotel?" Kraft asked, as we got up. "It's teeming outside."

"Thanks, my friend, but that's all right," said Dad cheerfully. There was no way we could afford any hotel, let alone this one. "We want to move on a bit before we stop for the night."

In fact, we stopped at the nearest campsite in the downpour and decided to sleep in the station wagon. That meant Dad had to transfer everything from the back — tent, suitcases, boxes of food, camping table and chairs — to the top of the car and cover it with a tarpaulin, in the dark. For once though, as he did so, we were all laughing. It was unforgettable: my drenched father swearing, the rest of us huddled under a tree, until he finally got it all stacked on top and folded down the back seats to make a bed. When I stretched out across the front seats to sleep, I banged my head on the steering wheel, so changed sides and banged my knees. My parents and brother managed to cram themselves into the back. Dave said sleepily that he had to pee, so Dad opened the back door of the car from the inside and pointed him out.

It could have been terrible, but it was funny.

And at the next campsite in France, there was a Volkswagen bus filled with English boys! I dreamed it was the Beatles and their crew, off for a secret vacation; Paul would come over to borrow some bread, and Dad would discover how much he liked their music and them ...

WHEN WE GOT back to Paris, we had to unpack and clean up, Mum and I of course doing most of the work. She told me my brother was going to be sent to stay with Jacques and his family at their country place — like me, shipped off to the middle of nowhere to improve his French, but he was only ten. It surprised me that Dad would do something like that to Dave. And then Mum dropped her bombshell.

"I hope it's all right, dear," she said, on her way out of the kitchen. "I'm going to London in a few days, to get away and visit Ma and Pa."

Speaking of problems!

"What about me?" I followed her around, begging her to let me come with her, not to leave me alone with my father. A whole week of "Sarah Heartburn, the Tragic Queen." And "Stop slumping and stand up straight, *nom de dieu*!" Telling me I was not Veronica Lake, to push my hair out of my face. Dad said I was a silly prude because I didn't like to see him walking around without any clothes on. My friends thought it was amazing that I'd often seen my dad naked. But I always made sure to shut my eyes or turn away. Between his legs was a purplish dangling thing I did not want to see or know what it was for. My experienced older friend at school, Nancy, had hinted that one day I might not feel that way about penises. But I could not imagine that feeling ever changing.

Mum said, "Don't worry, dear. He's always much nicer to you when I'm not around."

What a surprising thing to say. Poor Mum. Did she, I wondered, have an inferiority complex? As if it was her fault Daddy was mean to me? But how could anything be her fault?

My mother was adorable. All our friends said that. She was movie-star beautiful; people compared her to actresses I didn't know — Greta Garbo, Ingrid Bergman, Lauren Bacall. Mum had a soft English voice, and she was good at everything around the house — making jam, sewing, knitting — though her cooking definitely needed improvement. She painted watercolours and made music and pottery and a warm comfortable home, was loving to animals and to her garden and to us, especially when we were sick. She was a member of the Voice of Women — ladies who got together to agitate for peace.

But though it was hard to admit, there was another woman no one outside the house ever saw, one who was not good at keeping her feelings to herself, or at letting any of us live our own lives. It was my job to listen when that other mother criticized my dad. Though sarcastic sometimes, Dad never said a bad word about Mum, but she told me lots and lots of bad stuff about him.

The other, annoying mother drove me crazy with her dithering. She could never make up her mind about the simplest thing without asking everybody within ten miles their opinion, which she paid no attention to in any case. And she cried at everything, especially animals — if there was a kitten in a basket or a baby bird on a branch, my mother would be sobbing. Every animal on the street was, without doubt, lost. She'd spot a happy hound, loping along the streets of Halifax. "Gord, Gord, stop, oh look at that poor dog, he's lost."

My father would roll his eyes and keep on driving. I hated that he rolled his eyes. But I did too. Sometimes I thought my mother wept and was fearful because she was so sensitive, but other times — I hardly dared think it — I thought she was just silly.

The first time I remembered meeting the secret mother was just after David's birth. I had been caught behind the sofa, punching holes with a pencil in a photograph of Mum with her sisters, and she dragged me into the bathroom to shout at me, fingers digging into my arm. I stood frozen, staring up at the face with glittering eyes and furious mouth. At that moment, I knew I'd try very hard never, ever, to provoke that woman again.

But now I was a teenager and had no choice. Now she drove me mad. Except for the times when I fell in love with her, and she didn't.

THE FIRST NIGHT it was just the two of us, Dad said, "There's a film you should see, Bethie," and he took me to an American movie, *One Potato, Two Potato*, in English. It was about a tragic couple in the south of the United States, a Negro man and a white woman who fall in love and marry and face terrible racial prejudice. I found the film thought provoking and sad, almost as good as *To Kill a Mockingbird*, one of the best movies I'd ever seen. On the drive home, Daddy and I talked about how unjust segregation was in the South and the battle for civil rights.

"The white judge in the movie said that prejudice is wrong but can't be ignored," my father snorted. "Typical. That means, 'Though we know prejudice is wrong, we must yield to it, because we have no morality, no ethics and no guts.' The basis of racism. Hitlerism."

"Daddy, remember the time Hilly took me to the Waeg on a guest pass?" I asked. "I was furious the whole time, looking at those people having fun in the swimming pool and on the tennis courts. How could they possibly hate someone and not let them in because they're a Negro or a Jew?"

"People are closed-minded, Pupik," Dad said. "I'm fond of the human race, but we're petty, cowardly and blind. It's a good thing we have Wolfie Mozart to remind us how magnificent homo sapiens can be."

"The Beatles too," I said.

"Cats in heat," he said. But he was smiling.

"It said in the news," I said triumphantly, "that the Beatles refused to sing in Jacksonville, Florida, unless Negroes could sit wherever they wanted in the audience."

"Well well." He sounded impressed. "Good for them."

There was hope.

My dad didn't just talk about integration and justice — he lived those values and made us live them too. His friends and colleagues came from all over the world. At twelve, I'd been a bridesmaid for our good friend Peter, from Ghana.

That same summer, 1962, we went to visit my mother's oldest sister and her family in Washington, D.C., and there was a heat wave. One boiling afternoon, as we sat around gasping for air, my aunt suggested a trip to the local swimming pool, and Dave and I and my two cousins piled into their station wagon for Dad to drive us. But when we arrived, a picket line had surrounded the building. A row of Negro children and grown-ups were marching slowly back and forth in front of the entrance to the pool, carrying signs saying, *Unfair!* and *Down with segregation.* Dad went out, spoke to the marchers and brought us back one of the leaflets they were carrying.

"This is a segregated pool," he said. "We can't go in."

"Awww," we all whined. "No fair!"

"What's not fair is being forbidden to swim because of the colour of your skin," replied my dad.

My cousins were peeved, and so was I. What did their problem have to do with us? We were hot and wanted to cool down in the pool. Let them find their own pool! Dad said to my cousins,

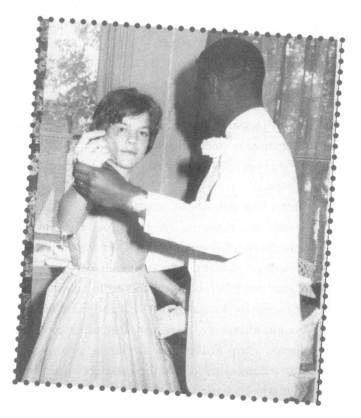

"If you want to go in, girls, I can't stop you, but my children will not cross that line."

Instead Dad took us to Baskin-Robbins, a huge ice cream parlour we did not have in Canada, and let us have two-flavour double-decker ice cream cones. Now, remembering Washington, I was ashamed. If I'd had the choice, I might have pushed right past those children in the picket line to have my refreshing swim with all the other white people. I'd thought only about how cool the water would be, not the injustice of being kept out. I was proud of my dad.

"It's good," I said, as we stopped at our Gentilly *boulangerie* to buy some delicious bread and a *pain au chocolat* for me, "to see movies that make you think."

MY FATHER HAD to go to work every day, so I had lots of time for writing. Lists of names trailed over the pages of my notebook, all of them sublime:

Mrs. Beth McCartney.
Mrs. P. McCartney.
Mrs. Elizabeth McCartney.

"But I just can't go, that's all, Paul!"

"But Beth, we'll have a marvellous time there! Swimming, horse back riding, tennis ... everything."

"But I can't!"

"Why not? Blimey. We went where you wanted to go last summer, and I'm going here this summer, if you want it or not! Beth, don't cry!"

He looked at me, distressed.

"I'm sorry Paul, I can't," I wept. "I'm four months pregnant."

"You're going to have a baby?" he asked, eyes pop-ping out.

I nodded tearfully. He took me into his arms, speechless, his "camp" already forgotten.

"A son," he murmered. "I'll teach him guitar."

I wrote to Mum.

We're getting on fine. Except for the fact that sometimes he spoils everything by insisting I do (ugh) Geometry, we haven't had too many unpleasant thoughts regarding one another.

Don't worry or hurry back. I know you're having great long talks with Granny, pouring out your troubles! Go to it.

And to Hillary.

All the mags say that Paul drives a green Goodwood. For heaven sakes, what sort of car is a Goodwood? They say Ringo drives a Ford Zodiac, so I guess he sold his Mini-Morris! George drives a Jaguar sports car, doesn't he? Mum said Paul's got nice handwriting — his is the best, and Ringo's is the worst.

If it weren't for you, kiddo, I'd be in a Beatle-less vacuum, so please keep sending interviews and pics! Dig?

Two nights later, after an hour of geometry and suffering, Dad took me to see *Tom Jones*, a movie that was restricted to eighteen and older back home and wasn't allowed to be shown at all, I'd heard, in Alberta. I loved it and tried not to be shocked by the sex. As a modern girl, I felt I shouldn't be shocked, though I'd never seen anything like it. It was so full of sex. Tom was jumping into bed with everyone, but also sweet and very handsome. Albert Finney, so masculine and yet so endearing with that impish grin, almost displaced Paul in my heart. For one minute.

Dad took me to a sidewalk café afterwards, and I asked questions. I didn't understand the scene where Tom and a woman were eating slowly, making such a mess with food dripping down and ending up in bed, or why Tom chased so many girls when he really loved only one. Dad gave a complicated answer about "the force of male desire" that I didn't listen to, but I did listen when he moved on to homosexuals and prostitutes. He told me about a nearby *club feminine*, a place for lesbians, and other strange places in Paris where strange people can go, like those who take pleasure in hurting themselves or others. There were long, scientific-type names for these people. It made me feel excited and grown-up to talk about such interesting things with my father. *Dad was describing "fettishists" and "sado-masicists" etc.*, I wrote late that night. *My horizins are broadening!*

I DIDN'T TELL my father about my own experience with a kind of strangeness, at Camp Arcady when I was eleven, the only year I went to summer camp. The evening I arrived, the older campers presented *Patience,* a Gilbert and Sullivan musical, with the boy hero played by an American counsellor called Lily. I fell madly, passionately in love with the character in the musical, and then with Lily herself; I'd go beet red and tremble when she was near. Being me, of course, I couldn't keep my crush to myself, so everyone knew and teased me and called me "lezzy." I wondered if I really was a lezzy.

But that never happened again. From then on, I just liked boys. What a relief. It was bad enough in Halifax being half-Jewish and getting good marks and all that without being a lezzy too.

I wrote to all my friends at home about the movie and the chat with Dad, sure none of them had had that kind of frank talk with their dad. Hillary wrote back that the girls in my class had founded The Sex Club: to get in, you had to tell the others, in detail, what you'd do with your husband on your wedding night. It made me glad to be far away, because I'd have flunked my membership test. Lea wrote that she was madly in love with Roger Moore, the Saint.

What about poor John?!!! I wrote. *How can you be so fickle? I will never abandon Paul for anyone, ever.*

I didn't mention my very brief crush on Albert Finney. She didn't need to know about that.

❦

I KNEW SO little about sex. Books were baffling. I'd once sneaked an exotic-looking book of Dad's called *The Second Sex* to school, and the girls had gathered around to look for the good bits. The writer, some French woman, did mention prostitutes, lesbians and intercourse, but her book was disappointingly serious and dull. *Women in Love* by D.H. Lawrence, an English author, had a promising title but was truly tedious, with characters getting all het up, ranting on and on about nothing — a waste of time. I couldn't finish that one.

I also didn't finish a book I found at home called *The Group*. There was a scene near the beginning where a girl arrives at a man's apartment. They make love, and then afterwards they lie in the bed while he smokes a cigarette. As if he's surprised, the man looks at the girl and says, "You came!"

And I thought, "Of course she CAME, she's right beside you. You couldn't have gone to bed with her if she weren't there!"

I wished there were someone to explain these things to me, as Nancy used to. Nancy was an older girl I hung around with for a while. My mother said Nancy was common. She was not common; in fact, she was quite unusual. She was stacked, for one thing, and she was fast. She knew lots about boys and sex, even more than Carol next door, who before Jimmy had had a real boyfriend in Saskatoon. Nancy told me, "When you're petting, you make sex juice." I nodded as if I understood, but really, she could have been speaking Chinese.

When Nancy informed me that intercourse meant the man's penis poking right up into the woman, the thought was so repulsive I decided she must be joking. It couldn't possibly be right. I did my best to imagine some other way — maybe it was the other bit, the balls part my father called his marble bag, which fitted in somehow. Because how could that pointy thing feel good, stabbing away inside you?

But by now, I'd guessed her version must be true. There were new feelings in my own body, surges, urges ... I began to think I was a sex maniac. Something was going on down there.

I mean, something more than usual.

I was very young when I learned there was a place down there that felt good. Not all the time, but at certain times it felt good. How perfect that we were designed so when we lay in bed, our arms reached just that far.

Before, I'd only considered that part of my body for what it was not. It was not a peeny — my mother's name for what my brother had. Dave and Dad could wave theirs around and use it to pee standing up; more than once, when we were out walking in the woods in winter, my father had tried to pee the word "Beth" in the snow, though he only ever had enough pee for three letters. Was that convenience and freedom why their private thing was so much better than what I had, which Mum called a popo and was hidden? Girls had to sit down. When camping, this was really inconvenient.

Nancy and I were talking on the phone once when she said the word "masturbate." I put the phone down and ran to get the dictionary.

"You don't even know what it means," she said.

"I do so, I'm just checking," I said. So it had a name! I was relieved. That meant other people did it too.

Now I was curious about actual sex, which meant doing things with men — going all the way. But at the same time, I did not want to know what was really involved, the neck sucking and poking and such. I was happy lying in bed at night, holding hands with myself, pretending it was Paul.

DADDY TOOK ME to wander along the Seine, where we browsed at the *bouquinistes* — the booksellers whose stores were big boxes attached right to the walls beside the river. He loved very old, mildewed books with gold letters on leather bindings, and I loved all books except some of the ones I saw there, with titles like *1000 Questions about Sex with 25 Colour Pictures* and *The Art of Kissing — Full Instructions*. Also *Nature* magazine, which was like the new men's magazine *Playboy*, only with no clothes at all. Women *entirely devoid of clothing*. I was scandalized.

Then there was a book I happened to pick up and begin to read that made me feel ill after a few lines. It was filthy — much worse than *The Carpetbaggers* or *Lolita* or *Lady Chatterley's Lover* that Dad had and I'd taken a peek at once or twice. This one was called *The Naked Lunch*, and it took the cake. I wrote to Hilly to warn her that if she saw this book, she should run away. It was sick.

Hillary sent shocking news: a young woman in Germany had accused Paul of being the father of her baby! So Paul wasn't an innocent choirboy, as I'd wanted to believe. I replied bravely it was fine with me that he was not a virgin. What twenty-two-year-old man could go through life liking only *jelly babies*?

Anyway, sometimes at night, Paul and I were starting to try other things. He had curious hands that wanted to know me better, and I liked what he did.

My rival for his love, horrible Jane Asher, who the magazines said was still Paul's girlfriend, was much on my mind. I had no doubt that she was a gold-digging alcoholic, stringing Paul along, interested only in his fame and money. This repulsive drunk began to appear regularly in my stories.

While Dad was at work, I sat all day in the silent apartment reading and writing, including a scrumptious story in which Paul and my twenty-year-old self were both dating other people — he the vulgar Jane Asher and I some guy called Andy — when we met by chance at a café and fell instantly in love.

I'm 20 years old. Physically, if my friends aren't lying, I'm pretty enough, and sexy. No, I'm not conceited, I just am attractive. That's the way I was born. But I'm not a Beautiful Bubblehead; I've just finished university with a B.A. Anyway, there's my case.

The story takes place in a very dusky, smoky, noisy club/café. I must say, I was at my best that night, in a very low-cut blouse and tight skirt with my suede jacket and slingbacks, and my hair flipped slightly. Andy and I sat there, enjoying the scene. Our peace was interrupted by a drunk young woman with bangs so low she could hardly see anything and a dress so low we could easily see everything, who sat down beside Andy.

Suddenly I saw, threading his way through the crowd, one of the most handsome men I have ever seen. He was very tall, his clothes faintly disorderly but style-wise perfect — tapered pants and Cuban heels, very a la mode. He had a thick head of fairly long hair,

and his eyes were merry and rimmed with lashes.
  I gave him a thourough once-over and could have
fallen adoring at his feet.
  He was the boyfriend of the horror next to Andy.

At the end, as Paul and I whirled away in a dance, he invited me to go with him to Liverpool.

Take me there please, I prayed. Just take me there.

ONE OF DAD's young New York cousins arrived in Paris, and the three of us went out to dinner. Robert was twenty-seven, handsome and mature. I got dolled up — backcombed and sprayed my hair and put on the padded bra with a bit of foam fibrefill, the pink flannel shift Mum had made, my fishnet nylon stockings with a dark diamond pattern and my gold heart locket with the tiny picture of Paul cut to fit one side and of our dachshund Brunhilda on the other. I slipped on my new shoes with the Baby Louis heel. Mum and I had fought, again: I still wanted an illusion or a jet heel, and she would allow only a Baby Louis heel, because of my height, she said. What height? I was growing, yes, but normally, not like HER height. Though my feet were getting worryingly big, size nine already. I prayed, please God, do not give me kangaroo feet like my mother's.

When I walked into the living room, Daddy said, "Where's my little Pupikina?" and Robert said, "Va va voom!"

"All grown up," Robert continued. "Last time I saw you, you were a little girl."

"Thank you. I like a casual but sophisticated look," I replied, smoothing my hair.

The restaurant was a chic little haunt of Dad's bygone days. He told us about volunteering for the American Army during the war and being sent to do basic training in Oxford, England, where one weekend he went to a Chopin recital, saw a stunning, very tall Englishwoman and introduced himself to her — luckily for me and Dave, because it was our mother. They discovered that they both loved and played classical music, went on a date where they listened to late Beethoven string quartets on a record player Dad had borrowed, and fell madly in love. If this weren't a story about my parents, it would have been romantic.

And then he talked about moving on with his unit to Paris, where he fell madly in love with everything French. After the war, he stayed in Paris for a year and took classes at the Sorbonne, where he met his buddy Jacques and saw my mother again. It was hard to think of my dad so young. He seemed a bit more human when he spoke about his memories, which he almost never did. Dad had told me that when he saw the movie *Dr. Strangelove*, he'd wept with laughter. I couldn't imagine him weeping, even for fun.

Robert offered me a sip of his wine, but I didn't like it — too sour. It was easy in French restaurants to eat in a grown-up way, because you could order *steak frites* — no vegetables, just meat and the most delicious chips. Daddy ordered pig's ear, a rare delicacy, he boasted, but even he was taken aback when it arrived sitting upright on a bed of lettuce, looking just like a pig's ear on a bed of lettuce. He ate every bit and said it was delicious. Natch.

A photographer wanted to take our picture for money; Dad said no, but Robert said he'd pay so we'd have a souvenir. This was what I'd dreamed of in Halifax — having my picture taken in a Paris bistro with two grown men, one of them twenty-seven and debonair. Too bad he was my father's cousin, and the other was my father.

Best of all, as we left the café, the waiter said, "*Au revoir, Madame.*" As if he thought I was Dad's wife. It made me laugh. I wrote to tell Mum about that.

AT HOME, AFTER carefully rolling down and putting away my nylons, I listed what was next in my journey to womanhood, the milestones that lay ahead:

1. *my first two-piece bathing suit*
2. *my first scant bikini*
3. *my first floor-length gown*
4. *my first date*
5. *my first kiss (sigh)*
6. *my first steady boy*
7. *my first (well, six years later perhaps) proposal*
8. *my first engagement (actually, I don't plan to have many more!)*
   etc.

The next day, taking the laundry down from the line and folding it, feeling very mature, I picked up Mum's lacy pink nightgown, slipped it on over my clothes and pretended to be a glamorous nightclub singer, crooning "Till There Was You" into a little saucepan. So much for mature.

On our last stroll by the Seine, Dad said I could pick some books, any books. He usually had strong opinions about what I read: he'd tried to stop me reading *The Lion, the Witch and the Wardrobe*, the whole Narnia series, because he said it was Christian propaganda. I adored those books and read them all anyway, over and over. Yes, Aslan was a noble, wise leader who sacrificed himself for the good of his people. Did that mean I'd think he was Jesus Christ and rush to get baptized? Give me a break, Dad. Aslan was a LION.

Now my father trusted me more. I picked four used paperbacks — an Agatha Christie, a Jeeves, an Ellery Queen and *Wuthering Heights*.

"I really liked *Jane Eyre*, so I can't wait to read this," I said.

"You dear thing," he said. "It's terrific you're such a reader."

We had tea in a café while it rained, and when the sun came back out, we sauntered around the inside of Notre Dame Cathedral. Gaping at that stunning stained glass window in the middle, the light shining through to design, on the floor, a glittering tumble of emeralds, rubies and sapphires, I felt myself bursting with joy at being in Paris. Paris! The most beautiful city in the world!

Except for Halifax.

Dad said, "Let me feel my bumps."

He and I got along really well the entire week, not one single fight, not even an argument. I actually cooked him supper once — scrambled eggs, which he said were superb. That was a relief, since that was the only thing I knew how to cook.

"Brava!" he said, licking his plate. Happily washing the dishes that night, I pretended to be a housewife, tidying my very own kitchen. Even if it was mouldy, it was mine.

When I was married, taking care of Paul would be my job. Nothing would matter more.

DAD HAD TO drive into the country to bring Dave back. He asked if I wanted to come, but instead I got to stay alone in the apartment for two whole days, eating toast and Shreddies and taking long baths, reading *Wuthering Heights* and writing. I was too nervous to go outside. Didn't need to anyway. I was in heaven all by myself. *I'll become a hermit in later years, I think,* I wrote.

Dad and David came back from the country, and Mummy came back from London, and just like that — I couldn't believe it, and yet I could — the nagging started, and the fighting. Daddy started whacking again. Was that peaceful interlude a dream? When it was the two of us, he was hugs and kisses, "dear thing" and feeling my bumps. The next minute, with the other two there, he was a snapping, snarling beast, like Heathcliff. He said I was rude, filthy, crazy. Yes, crazy.

"What a pampered brat you are," he sneered.

"You liked me last week when we were alone," I wanted to shout. "What did I do wrong?"

No point asking. I just moved out of his way.

Mum: "Beth, your hair's getting too long, you need a hair cut."

Me: "I like it the way it is."

Dad: "Never mind what she wants. Don't ask her, just send her to the hairdresser."

THINGS WERE BACK to normal with Mum too: "Wash your face." "Comb your hair." "Take your elbows off the table." "Put your hair out of your eyes." "Pick up your clothes." "You are not wearing that!"

My insides closed down, like a book slamming shut. I curled

up between the covers, where they couldn't get me. Why was my life like this?

Because I was unlovable.

September 18

I use Paul when I feel depressed or very angry. That's another use for a person you love — a straw to clutch at, that turns out to support you beautifully. Someone who you can remember in bad moments, whose memory will pull you through. A boy so you can say, "What does it matter if Mum is being so unfair and mean? Paul loves me, he'll always be there. I'll be seeing him soon."

And the thought of him and his love will make your heart swell with joy till you think you'll burst with happiness. Now do you see why I have Paul? I try to say to myself that it's silly to be depressed, there's always Paul — but what is Paul? He'll never know me, he's 2000 miles away. My Paul is a dream, a beautiful dream, a ghost. When I grab at this straw, it's usually too watery and wispy to hold me up. I know it's full of holes, and so I sink.

But I still had the memory of *One Potato* and *Tom Jones* and "Brava." The photograph in my room — Dad and Robert leaning on the checkered tablecloth, and me, casual and sophisticated in my fuzzy pink shift.

9

※※

September

A real French girl introduced herself to me by the elevators in our apartment building and told me, in bits of English, that my father had run into her and suggested she find me. Her name was Hélène, she loved the Beatles and she had a record player. I was saved! Though only temporarily, because she was moving away before long. When her family went out, I dashed to her place with my records, we listened in her living room and danced, and I felt wonderfully normal for an hour or two. She was another George girl — the quiet type.

She came to my place and we went through my pictures, picking our favourites. She told me an unbelievable story: that the Beatles had played in Paris that very January, and *lots of people didn't like them.* My jaw dropped. How typically French to see the most fab thing on Planet Earth and give it the brush-off.

Hélène had taught herself English through the titles of pop songs. When it got late, she said, "Now I must go" (The Swinging Blue Jeans). I said no, and we began to play-wrestle. "You've really got a hold on me," she said (Beatles), then "Hold me tight!" (Beatles) When I pinned her down, she cried, "Not a second time" (Beatles) and "Don't bother me" (Beatles).

I said, "*Tu es folle.*"

"Thank you girl," she replied (Beatles).

Hélène ran over to tell me that their movie *A Hard Day's Night* had at last come to France, and we made a date to go as soon as possible. Its title was translated as *Quatre garçons dans le vent* — four boys in the wind. What in the name of Paul did *that* mean?

On the day we were supposed to go to the movie, my mother said first I had to hem a skirt that was too long. After what felt like hours of work, she forced me to tear it out and start again, nagging about sloppy work and seam binding.

Question: What on earth is more useless than seam binding?

Answer: Nothing.

But at last she let me go. We took the metro to the Champs-Elysées and dashed into the Triomphe Cinema, only five minutes late.

It was fabulous, clever, as gear as gear could be. I couldn't believe I was seeing giant close-ups of the faces I adored, hearing those precious Liverpool accents. Paul was so very sweet, but George too, and John, though he was portrayed as a sarcastic jokester, and Ringo the melancholy scapegoat. I sat tapping my feet, waving my hands in time, my whole body fizzing with melody and passion and delight. It was the story of the Beatles leaving on a train and their pranks before appearing on a TV show. George had to judge some grotty shirts, Ringo went parading solo, John splashed fully clothed in a bathtub, adorable Paul scolded his trouble-making grandfather, and they played fantastic music all the way through. One song in particular, "And I Love Her," was so tender and heartfelt, it made me feel as though my skin was being peeled off.

"She gives me everything," Paul sang.

Yes Paul, I thought, I do. Or at least — I will.

And one scene, where they escaped from a rehearsal and ran outside to a big field, leaping, dancing in circles, flinging themselves about — such playfulness and humour, you could see what good friends they were, how much they enjoyed one another's company. Four nice young men with lots of talent who by great good fortune had met and become friends and band-mates and were having the time of their lives making music together.

How very lucky we are, I thought, to be part of it all.

Hélène adored the movie too. It was funny to see the French attempt a translation at the bottom — I wondered how they'd translate "gear" and "fab" and "lummy." We saw it twice — it was expensive, eight francs, $1.60, so we got our money's worth — and could have watched it twenty times again, especially "And I Love Her." I wanted to wrap myself in Paul's voice and never take it off.

What a let-down to leave that fine, rich world of music, laughter, perfectly gorgeous boys and love, head into the rain and descend to stinky Denfert-Rochereau to wait for the train back to Miseryland. While we stood on the wet black platform, I made up a story.

"The band came secretly to Paris for a holiday," I said to Hélène, "and one day I saw Paul, my very own Paul McCartney standing right here on this spot, at the Denfert-Rochereau station, staring puzzled at a map. Coolly, in a sophisticated yet casual way, I said, 'You look a bit lost. Can I help you?'"

"Thank you, girl," said Hélène.

"'Oh yes please,' said Paul with a grateful smile," I went on, "amazed that I spoke English and wasn't screaming, and I helped him find his way back to his hotel, where he invited me in to meet ... "

The train rumbled in.

"I'd be happy just to dance with you," said Hélène.

I CONCLUDED THE film review in my diary: *Oh Paul, Paul, Paul, you are the most heavenly person. HEAVENLY! So, so so SWEET. Yet gentle, sensitive — EEEEEEE!! I'm bursting.*

And I made a list of important Beatle words from the movie:

> *and all*
> *aye*
> *dead kinky*
> *anyroad*
> *old 'un*
> *, like*
> *'course*
> *right mixer (?)*
> *all that stuff*
> *shurrup*
> *you lot*
> *eh*
> *meself*
> *y'what!*
> *You've got ..., you have*
> *daft*

And swore to use them meself as often as possible and all that daft stuff, eh. Anyroad. In a picture Babs had sent of the boys having breakfast, Ringo was devouring a soft-boiled egg, George bacon and eggs, John toast and Paul — nothing. "Paul needs to eat more healthily," I said, showing it to Mum. "When we're married, I'll make sure he gets enough to eat."

"They've got the milk bottle on the table," was all she said. Typical snobby Mum remark, as if the Beatles cared about pouring their milk from a nice jug. Mum liked John best. Or George. Not Paul, since he was mine and all. 'Course.

Sept. 17

*Tonight Mum came in to talk. All day I was concious of
myself trying to shove her off, push her away. Family meals
are an agony to me now. My room is my haven, where the
secluse can be secluded. She asked me what was wrong. During
the ensuing conversation we both were dissolved into tears, as
usual. I felt so many emotions at one time.*

    *I have a theory — a teenager is basicly selfish, watching
over and caring for herself alone — for the moment everybody
else doesn't exist, isn't important. All of a sudden, she sees
herself change, she begins to have problems etc., and she
becomes absorbed.*

If only parents could understand the needs of the secluse.

HILLY SENT A funny newspaper clipping: some professor named
McLuhan, speaking to a Conservative party conference at home,
had said, "Nobody would expect me to address a group of
politically thoughtful people without referring to the Beatles." The
Conservative party! He told them political parties "must begin to
think about their responsibilities to the teenager." One of the old
guys interrupted, "Are you suggesting that Mr. Diefenbaker get a
Beatle hairdo?"

I showed it to Dad, and we had a good chuckle — a Beatle
wig on the crinkled head of old Dief the Chief, with his
turkey wattles. Dad informed me that he'd read all the reviews
of the Beatles' movie, French and otherwise, and was unable to
find an unfavourable one, so he was seriously thinking of
seeing it.

I didn't believe him.

September 19, Saturday

I have a funny feeling again. I want, I long, to draw something beautiful, or write or dream something beautiful, or to be beautiful. Why? I don't know.

Anne Frank talks about longing — so longing — for everything, and feeling utterly confused. "I don't know what to read, what to write, what to do, I only know that I am longing!"

These lines apply perfectly to me.

❦

GETTING TO MY new school was an ordeal — the suburban line to Denfert, then one metro, changing to another, and a bus. My first day, Mum came with me, and it took an hour.

Almost all French schools were girls or boys only, but Dad had found a special *lycée pilote*, an experimental French high school where boys and girls actually went to school together. Welcome to the real world, stick-in-the-mud France. I'd been going to an all girls' school for three years; it was dazzling that first day to see hunks of maleness sitting at the desks. We were in the international section of the school, specifically for kids from elsewhere — South America, Israel, the United States, Japan, the Philippines, Cambodia. Only me from Canada. There was a Houl, an Emmanuel, a Talma, a Chenian, a Sakamoto.

But I was disappointed; there were no dream boys. They were all square — white socks, short hair, square. The Israelis Zev, Oded and Schlomo were the nicest; their names were strange, but the three of them were funny and friendly. Unfortunately, absolutely not Beatle-type cute. I made friends with Susan from St. Louis, Missouri, whose father was in the diplomatic corps and who loved Ringo, which I tried not to hold against her. She agreed with me that four math classes a week were three too many. The amount of time we spent at school and then doing homework was ridiculous. I was pleased that we could wear slacks to school whenever we wanted — no slacks allowed in my school at home, even on the snowiest days. But otherwise — yech.

The best part of the school day, unbelievably, was lunch, a hot meal that started with a little snack called an *ordoove* — tuna fish or cucumbers or paté, to fill us up, I guessed, so we didn't eat too much of the main meal. Which was meat or fish — roast chicken or steak and chips, always fish on Fridays — and vegetables. Then there was a salad and then cheese and then a dessert, such as ice cream. When we sat down, there were baskets of fresh bread, cut from those sticks of great French bread called *baggets*, just sitting on the table, and the drink sometimes was juice and sometimes beer — yes, beer! The kids at home couldn't believe that. And I who didn't like strange food was so hungry by lunchtime that I ate everything on my plate, except the day we had tongue and I could see the taste buds. We ate some stringy meat that I didn't find out till later was horse meat; that also did not make me happy.

The worst part of the school day — there were lots of worsts, endless math and in English, groan, we were doing *Macbeth* AGAIN — was gym class. We were supposed to climb ropes, of all things. The other kids, even the girls, just grabbed the rope and shimmied right up. I got about a foot off the ground before I stopped. I wasn't going to burn my legs on that rope, and anyway, my arms and legs weren't strong enough, and it was too high up there. The teacher bawled me out and tried to help, and I "accidentally" stood on her hand. I was not climbing that rope.

What was the point of sports? Running around getting sweaty and trying to beat someone. My mother loved sports. At home, she wanted me to learn tennis, so we could play together. "I spent endless hours of my childhood," she'd often told me, "hitting a tennis ball against the school wall." As if that sounded like a good idea. Like fun. She had registered me for tennis lessons so I could be her personal school wall. Back and forth, wham wham, what for?

Even simple sports where you didn't need lessons, like skating or tobogganing, were just too scary and fast for me. In a skating race at the Ladies College, I came in second last, just ahead of my classmate Gladys who had fallen out of a car onto her head when she was small and was mentally retarded. You had to be unbelievably slow to be just ahead of Gladys.

Toboggans were especially frightening, all that downhill speed. Though at least tobogganing was a winter sport Dad could do with us. When I was a year old, Dad's legs and arms had been completely paralyzed by polio. It was a miracle, Mum said, that the virus stopped just before paralyzing his lungs, or he would have been in an iron lung or dead. He was alive due to the force of his will, because he simply refused to die. And he could walk because, against the advice of his doctors, he had made himself exercise.

Still, he'd lost so much muscle, he could never again ski or run or skate. But he could whiz down a hill on a sled. Not that he did very often. We'd seen a home movie of him when he was a kid in New York, tobogganing in Central Park after a snowstorm. He was of course the most rambunctious of the boys my grandpa was filming with his new movie camera. In those days, my father could run, even in the snow.

We never talked about what Dad could and couldn't do; we simply never went skiing like other families. I didn't want to anyway. Who wanted to strap pieces of wood to your feet and hurtle down a mountain at a hundred miles an hour, only to crash into a tree? In the freezing cold?

Though — there was a moment, once. We were playing basketball in gym class at the Ladies College, and my body was taken over by the spirit of someone else, someone fierce and determined with powerful legs and a big pumping heart. It wasn't that I wanted to win. I wanted to run. I ran all over the court, defending, all speed and strength. "I love this," I thought, my breath coming fast as I darted back and forth, keeping Janice from passing the ball. "I love this!"

Miss Willis, the bulky gym teacher with the big whistle, had never said anything to me before except "Get a move on, Elizabeth." But this time, she said, "Excellent work. That's a side of you we haven't seen before. Keep it up."

But it never happened again. The girl who didn't want to move came back. That feeling in my stomach — it'll hurt if I get up. It was like sinking in the mud, frozen, impossible to get out. Sitting in a chair reading and writing was all that mattered.

Plus who would want to go out with a girl who was not only flat-chested and good in school but competitive and sweaty? I would not be climbing any stupid French ropes.

WE WERE ASSIGNED a book report. I decided on *Sons and Lovers* by D.H. Lawrence because the hero's name was Paul, though his Paul had a moustache and mine was way nicer. Lawrence wrote *Lady Chatterley's Lover* and was, I'd heard, a homo. But then the stuffy English teacher said I couldn't use that book. Typical. I did Hemingway instead, *A Farewell to Arms*, which was a very lovely book.

Amazingly, two boys — Mario from the Philippines and Houl from Cambodia — seemed to like me. They both asked me to go for a Coke after school. A first — someone inviting me out! No one I liked had ever invited me anywhere — the reverse, in fact. In grade five, I'd overheard Scott, the king of my heart in grades four, five and six, invite my enemy Brenda to a party. "Sorry, Scott," she'd said, snickering. "I'm sure to be busy that night."

Poor guy! He was so cute, with his crew cut and pug nose, but he was poor, and Brenda was rich. I tapped him on the shoulder. "I'm free that night, Scott," I said. "I'll go with you." He looked as if he didn't see me and walked away. Hillary told my mother, and I got a lecture. "Never throw yourself at boys," Mum said. "They won't respect you if you're too eager."

That was all very well if you were gorgeous. But what if you'd waited three years for a boy to notice you, what then?

I was not captivating, like my beautiful mother. English Granny told me that when my mother was young and living in London, a man had sat down on a bus opposite her and noticed her and started to stare. When she got off the bus, he got off too and followed her all the way home, gazing at her like an adoring dog. He'd had to be sent away.

"Your mother has a come-hither look," Granny said, smiling.

I did not have a come-hither look. In fact, I had a go-away look. Why hadn't Mum passed on her magnetic skills to me? She adored men, and they her. My mother was a sorceress who could enchant people and make them do what she wanted.

But I could not, would not come on to people in that flirty way. I disliked seductive behaviour, and Paul did too.

Now boys were noticing me. But Mario and Houl were both finks. I said no.

LONG LETTERS TO and from my Halifax schoolmates sustained me. *My life is a continuous stream of problems, trains and hard work. I've even got blackheads now*, I wrote to Hilly. *I think*

*about what it'll be like when we're home and everything is normal
again. This year is like a dream. I don't mean "nice" like a dream,
I mean "unreal" like a dream.*

Hilly wrote back that the class had now formed the SMC —
the Sex Maniacs Club. And she'd read that the Beatles had
been to some kind of wild party in Hollywood, and John and
Paul were seen petting! Not with each other, of course. God!

I replied instantly. *We will disregard such sacreligious libel!*

OCCASIONALLY, THOUGH LIVING without newspapers or news
on the radio, I tried to keep up with current events. I was
delighted when Dad told me that an American Negro leader
called Dr. Martin Luther King had won the Nobel Peace Prize.
His award would surely help the cause of civil rights.

But mostly, I was interested only in me.

Le 22 octobre

*Wilson won the British election (the Beatles supported
him), the U.S. has by far outnumbered everybody in the
number of gold medals at the Olympics, Kruschev has
suddenly been ousted from the Russian government, and
John Lennon had his birthday October 9. (I forgot it.)
Pope Paul's in India and all. Big thrill. (I've just reread
"Catcher in the Rye" — it was great, but my vocabulary
has become more colloquial.)*

*I wonder if people will ever learn in History books
what I read in newspapers? Who knows, for in 20 years
time, there will surely be a more painless way of learning
than slogging away with a book — not that I ever did!
At school I feel I'm a failure, a flop and in a hole, and
I'm very discouraged. I've analysed another part of me,*

however — I would never (I hope) commit suicide,
because I feel that if one has a period of depression
and hardships, a spell of happiness will follow. It's like
Shakespeare — after a grim scene, a comical scene. Our
whole lives are like Shakespeare.

Oh dear, I really am all mixed-up! I don't know if I
love or despise my parents and I don't know if my parents
love or despise each other. My father doesn't have any
feelings whatsoever, my mother has too many.

And why must I be so loud and heard above everyone?
Why can't I be quiet even when I try to be? I'm twisted
outside–in or inside-out or something. I want a boyfriend,
I want to talk to my friends at home, I want to be happy
and I want a chocolate milkshake!

THEY MAY HAVE been finks, but even so, I was interested in what the boys thought of me, so in November, I organized a vote. We girls voted on the boys — best looking, funniest, coolest, best dressed — and invited them to do the same for us.

Some of my awards pleased me, and some did not. Not "Best Figure," of course, but I'd hoped to win "Nicest Eyes," which went to lovely Mika from Burma. So much for my greatest beauty asset. The first award they gave me, "Best Legs," was startling; I hadn't realized there was anything special about my legs. Unfortunately, what mattered was not nice legs but size of breasts, like in *Playboy*.

Then the boys handed me "Biggest Personality" and "Best Sense of Humour." Those were okay — though I was surprised a lowly Canadian had won over the self-confident American girls.

"Biggest Chin." I should have expected it, but it hurt. I hated having a chin so long, it was in a weather system all its own. And "Biggest Mouth" — well, I did not take this literally, as my actual mouth was quite small. But I was definitely noisy. See award #2.

In a rousing finale, the boys voted me "Craziest Beatlemaniac," "Most Neurotic" and "Must Go." Well — I was mad craziest for the Beatles, and I was just mad crazy. But their "Must Go" was not serious. I was sure the boys of the Lycée de Sevres found me loony but fun.

But I did go. At the end of term, Dad decided I was speaking too much English and not learning French, and he began to look for a regular French school. For once, I agreed with him; it did seem nuts to be in France speaking English all day with Susan from St. Louis, Missouri. And so, though I didn't want to switch, I didn't fight him as hard as I sometimes did. Besides, the *lycée pilote* was way too far, and there was too much math.

All I was sorry to leave, really, were Zev, Oded and Schlomo.

In my spare time, with no friends to play with, I kept busy reading and writing. In my stories now, Paul and I were of course together, but George Harrison was often secretly in love with me. Why George? Well, John was still married, and Ringo was Ringo. So that left George.

My absolutely favourite tale shared the writing paper with a bit of French vocabulary and last month's geometry homework.

GEORGE

"I can't stand it any longer, Beth." George looked at me beseechingly. "Please understand — I love you."

"Oh ... no," I murmered, stricken.

"Oh, I tried not to. But I saw you with Paul again and again and it wrenched my heart out. I tried to avoid you but Paul was always there, talking about you, praising you, asking us what he should buy you next, telling us

don't look so sad. I'm really sorry; I can love you as a brother and a good friend." "Can you? Really?" his face brightened. "Of course" I replied warmly. "Well, 'cause, sorry, all." His face still embarrassed, ... loped out. Paul was no longer angry, but pensive. I walked over and kissed him, then said, "I'm really sorry for George — I mean, he's all alone here in London, Paul, we have an extra room. Why can't he live with us?" "No. He isn't. He gets ideas again." He replied shortly. However, within 10 minutes, I had completely won him over, so I hurried out to tell George who looked very happy and ... "and that was how George came to live with us" ... when Paul and I kissed, or held hands or hugged he worried but he soon ...

what you'd said that day, describing what you wore, how wonderful you were. He loves you. And now — so do I."

"Oh, George, I don't ... I can't ... oh dear!" I turned to him, distressed. "But I don't love you, George. I love Paul."

"Oh, Paul. He doesn't know what love is. He's a choirboy, like they said. Affeminate and what's more ..."

I interrupted his bitter tirade with an angry look.

"Oh, I'm sorry." He sighed hopelessly. "Just remember, Beth — I love you."

Suddenly, another voice broke into our little talk — Paul's — furious.

"That's all very well, George, but she's my bird and she's marrying me. Get it?"

George rose to his feet, flushed and embarassed.

"I'm sorry Paul," he murmered in a low voice. "I didn't want to do anything wrong. I'll get over it."

"Oh, George. Please don't look so sad," I said. "I'm really sorry. I can love you as a brother and a good friend."

"Can you? Really?" His face brightened.

"Of course," I replied warmly.

"Well, s'cuse. Sorry, all."

His face still embarrased, he loped out. Paul was no longer angry, but pensive. I walked over and kissed him, then said, "I'm really sorry for George — I mean, he's all alone here in London. Paul, we have an extra room. Why can't he live with us?"

"No, he can't. He'd get ideas again," he replied shortly. However, within 10 minutes, I had completely won him over, so I hurried out to tell George, who looked very happy and murmered, "Gear."

And that was how George came to live with us. At first, when Paul and I kissed, or held hands or hugged, he winced, but he soon forgot.

Not one, but two Beatles. What a girl!

10

December

After school ended for the Christmas holidays, I had nowhere to go and nothing to do — no shopping centre, no pyjama parties, no phone calls. Lots of letters to Halifax, filled with stories and questions. *How in the name of Paul*, I wrote to Lea, *do you do the Frug, the Shimmy, the Watusi, the Mashed Potato, the Surf?* I was so far behind. How would I catch up?

Many long letters to Hillary.

> *Every time I think of Jane Asher, Hilly, I feel like throwing up. Once I got down one of my pix of Paul and punched him! Nearly broke my wrist! How can he love me when he loves her? When he talks about 'the girl I love,' do you think he means 'the girl I will love when I meet her' — or Jane? Grrr. I sometimes feel really queer when I think about him, in bed, for example. What would he be like? Priggish? Sexy? Choir-boy? Lord, what I'd give to know for sure!*
>
> *Men in France are very fresh, which I love. When in a café, they offer everyone a cigarette, including me! What a ball!*

*Around home, I seem to be more mature 'cause Mum
has no friends here so she tells her troubles to me.*

Just after a milk strike that meant we had to drink powdered
milk for ages, there was another national strike. This time, no
electricity or heating, no metros, no hot water. *They sure know
how to have a good time in this country*, I wrote to Hilly. Though
I had to admit — doing everything by the light of candles stuck in
wine bottles was cosy.

With my Christmas money, I bought a pair of baby blue stretch
pants so tight I could hardly breathe or walk. But my mother
didn't need to know that. Swanning around Galeries Lafayette,
I was thrilled to find out that my bra size in France was 85, which
sounded a lot better than 32, and that Barbie dolls and Clearasil
had both hit Paris. But not peanut butter. No peanut butter. And
yet, somehow, I was eating extremely well.

ONE LONG SNOWY day, shivering under blankets in my freezing
room, I wrote the best story, a long one that I could live inside for
days and days. I was a poor, beautiful orphan with waist-length
blonde hair when one morning, as I scurried across the street,
Paul accidentally knocked me down with his Aston-Martin sports
car. I was left paralysed with a broken back, and the orphanage
where I lived didn't want a cripple on its hands, so devastated
Paul moved me in with his parents. His mother wasn't dead in
the story, and as I lay helplessly in bed day after day, she and I
became very close.

One day gentle Paul reached over and gently took my hand.
And ... well, you know. Dreeeeam. Dreeeeeam dreeeeam dreeeeam.

*We became inseparable. When I graduated to a wheelchair,
there were wild rejoicings. And finally, at the age of 19, to*

*crutches. The doctor said that I should try to walk now, but
I was too afraid. Paul offered to help me, but I'd take one or
two hesitating steps and fall. Paul'd catch me and console me.*

*One day, Paul said that he was going downstairs for some
Coke. I heard him reach the top of the stairs, and then I heard
a terrible crash. "Paul!" I cried. No answer. I reached for my
crutches; they were too far away.*

*"Paul!" I screamed. No answer. My love and fear for him
overwhelmed me, and before I knew it, I walked, unsteadily,
but walked, to the top of the stairs. I saw him sprawled in a
heap at the bottom. Sobbing, I ran down and reached him.
I saw to my amazement and joy that his eyes were open, and
that he was smiling.*

*"You did it!" He sat up and hugged me. "You came to
me yourself!"*

We laughed and cried at the same time.

"I fell purposely!" he chuckled.

*Then he seemed to sober. He picked me up and laid me
on the sofa, then sat down and took my hands. His voice
became hesitant and gentler than ever.*

"Will you ... will you marry me?"

I flung my arms around his neck and kissed him.

"Yes, Paul," I cried. "And we'll <u>walk</u> together down the aisle!"

A luscious story like that could get me through anything. Even
Christmas vacation. In a Peugeot. With my family.

We spent part of the holidays driving around France in Dad's
station wagon. At home, if I had to drive around with them,
at least when the car stopped, I could jump out and get away.
Here, without much French, I didn't dare.

We were touring the boring Chateaux de la Loire. Big castles,
very old and very, very cold. Why didn't they have heat in those

days? It was colder inside than out; this was December, for God's sake. Everywhere we went, my mother read in her English accent from the green *Guide Michelin*. "*Un peu d'histoire ...*" she'd recite whenever we were getting near some history, which was every twenty-two seconds. She would actually turn around to the back seat, so Dave and I could hear better — as if we were listening. As if we were eagerly absorbing these fresh nuggets of French history.

Dave was reading *Tintin* comic books or dozing, and I had secretly brought my favourite reading material — the British fan magazines Babs had sent. I was getting worried about the Rolling Stones. There were rumours they were pushing out the Beatles; though the Fab Four had more top hits, it said the Stones had made more girls faint. I thought the Stones were all hideous, except Keith Richards who looked really sweet. One magazine said Mick Jagger was a Leo, like me. That meant, it said, that he was "generous, sympathetic, long-suffering, lucky in money matters, and at home in white, pale green, yellow and dark grey." That was definitely NOT me.

But it also said, "Mick can't stand phonies, is independent, can't tolerate discipline, has a strong will, can roar like a lion when in a temper, makes a good leader, is impetuous, has big nostrils and likes blue."

That WAS me. Too much.

With the Stones and many other groups, there was only one singer — one guy in front you looked at, the others in the background. With the Beatles, there were four singers, four strong voices, four big personalities. Though I personally only looked at Paul, fans had the option of looking at them all. Much better to have so much choice.

An interview with John Lennon in one mag almost made me laugh out loud; I had to stifle the sound, or Dad would get suspicious. Some really intelligent reporter commented to John on the frequent appearance of "her, me, you" in their songs.

John replied, "Well, what are we supposed to say? I Want to Hold *Its* Hand?"

I loved John — too bad he was married and a dad. I tried to imagine having John Lennon as my father. He wouldn't say his kid was a Neanderthal for liking pop music, that's for sure.

I read a story about a hundred-year-old woman who was asked if she liked the Beatles, and she said she didn't, they ruined her potato patch. I didn't get it for a minute — that someone, somewhere, didn't know who they were.

As I read one afternoon, my parents in the front seat were muttering about something called "the pill." Several times, after she was already in bed, Mum had asked me to bring her pills, tiny ones in a flat round container. I'd suspected they were some kind of birth control, and eavesdropping on my parents, it sounded like I was right.

Yech.

When we pulled up in front of the famous Château of Chenonceau with its famous turrets, my mother sat in the front seat reading *un peu d'histoire* from her *Guide Michelin*, and I sat in the back, poring over a list of the Beatles' favourite colours. Paul's was black. But this time, I wasn't ready; usually I'd hidden my reading material before we stopped. When Dad turned around, he saw what I was doing, reached over and yanked the magazine from my hands.

"You're going to look at this fucking chateau if it kills you," he said.

WE ALWAYS CELEBRATED Christmas, but every year there was a struggle. My father was allergic to Christmas. We never did any of the religious stuff, but still, something about a celebration of the birth of baby Jesus drove him mad. Mum had to push him out of the way to get the tree up and decorated and cook the traditional turkey dinner. This year he went on about wanting a stuffing made with oysters and chestnuts. Even thinking about this combination turned me green. Luckily, Mum ignored him. He didn't even realize he was making things difficult; he obviously relished the meal and watching us open our stockings and presents. But part of him was just snarky until we took down the tree.

We got lots of Christmas cards from our Halifax friends, each one precious. How tiny and safe Halifax seemed, way far away across the sea. I sent Hillary a gorgeous picture of Paul. On the back I wrote:

HOW TO WORK THIS PICTURE:

1. *Place against the wall*
2. *Light candles in front*
3. *Have lots of insense (insence? incense?)*
4. *Play "And I love her" softly in the background*
5. *Sway slowly, eyes closed, on knees before picture*

Voila. You will burst into uncontrollable shrieks of joy and imagine yourself married to Paul. Good luck!

Mrs. Beth McCartney.

Besides slippers and clothes, I was given a pile of books: *East of Eden* — I wanted to write like John Steinbeck; *A History of Mr. Polly* by H.G. Wells and *A Passage to India* by E.M. Forster, really good; a *Peanuts* book sent from Halifax. Best of all, my grandparents' present from London — the new Beatles LP,

Beatles for Sale, the British version of *Beatles '65*. Such a beautiful, serious picture on the front. Torture — Hélène had moved away, and I with no record player.

RINGO'S TONSILS GOT taken out. He recovered, which was a relief. He wasn't my favourite, but even so, he was the fourth most important person in the world.

ON BOXING DAY, Daddy found me in the living room, in tears.

"What's wrong, Bethie?" he asked. He usually did not notice when I was sad, but this holiday, he had been amazingly sweet to me for days. I told him I was really lonely and missed my friends. Dad sat down beside me, put his arm around my shoulder and gave me a squeeze.

"Matter and energy, my dear, that's all it is," he said in a kind voice. "Matter and energy."

I didn't know what that meant, but it was comforting, just the same. Daddy was a cell biologist who spent his life looking at life under a microscope. If you could not experiment on it, then, like God, it did not exist.

His words reminded me of when I was four years old and he'd come in to read a bedtime story. When Mum read, it was *Alice in Wonderland* or *Winnie the Pooh*. Dad liked those books too, but he preferred to read me a picture book of *The Iliad and the Odyssey*. In French. Even though the meaning of the story was a mystery, I loved having him close.

A BRAND NEW year was coming. *I'm as Beatle mad as I was a year ago, when I first discovered they existed*, I wrote in my diary. *A whole year of Beatle love, dreams, music, pictures, stories, magazines, books and spent money.*

Next year, Paul would find me.

1965

11

※◎※

January

January 1

*It's 1965 now; once again, time to live another year through.
I feel so tired and discouraged, my feelings are so changeable,
I go from one extreme to the other so quickly. Sometimes I
detest everything, I'm morose and somber and cheerless, I feel
trapped, closed in, wronged. I want most of all to escape from
the rule of my parents, obeying them, coming when they call,
eating when they want me to — it's sickening! If I were left
to myself, I'd do things when I wanted!*

  *In 1964 I was popular, fun-loving, lazy, disorganized,
shallow etc. Now my attitude to life is more cynical and
unhappy. I don't want to marry for I see what a rut my
mother is in and I feel that I'm too happy go-lucky to
accept the responsibility. However I expect (I hope) that
I'll have changed considerably by the time the question
may arise!*

The Lycée Claude Monet had huge wooden doors that creaked
when they were pushed open, like the doors of an old prison

in a movie. Early in January, I pushed through those doors and was shepherded into a classroom under the stares of thirty-eight French schoolgirls. Once I would have trembled at this ordeal, arriving at a strange school in a foreign language in the middle of the year. But now, I knew I could do this. Compared to a tent in a field in the French Alps, this was easy. The school had a roof.

The school secretary, my escort, introduced me to the teacher as *Elisabet, une Americaine.* Canada was never mentioned again. To them, I found out later, Canada was big, cold and uninteresting; America was where everyone wanted to be, even girls whose parents were Communists. From then on, I was *Elisabet l'Americaine,* and that was fine with me.

I sat in the class, completely lost as French flowed around me, and wondered if I'd ever make a single friend. When the bell clanged, my new classmates were eager to show me around, all the while checking out my shoes and clothes, grinning at my hesitant words of French. We were walking in a clump through the crowded halls when a very loud noise stopped us. A human foghorn stood bellowing in my path, jabbing a finger into my chest — a mean cement truck of a woman with a giant jaw who had taken an instant dislike to me, according to the rage on her face and in her voice. My classmates scrambled to explain who I was and why I wasn't answering her myself. But she shouted on as I stood looking at her, both of us stuck right there, face to face.

So I met Rosie the *surveillante,* whose job was to survey every second of the lives of the students of the Lycée Claude Monet and punish them for breathing. I found out there was an army of Rosies, the others younger and not as loud but just as powerful. It was like going through your school day surrounded by spies, who, if they caught you doing, saying, eating or wearing something wrong, gave you a *mauvaise note*. Every month you were marked out of twenty on conduct, and every *mauvaise note* — bad mark — got docked off your twenty. If you ever got zero for conduct, even once, you could not win any prizes, and the black stain followed you forever. It was terrifying, but only for a few days. After that, I realized that I just didn't care.

My misdeed the first day was that I wasn't wearing a *blouse*, a sort of beige lab coat we were all required to wear over our street clothes. It took my mother a few days to buy me one, and until my clothes were safely covered, I had to put up with deafening blasts from Rosie.

Day by day, I learned lots of other rules so incredibly petty I wanted to scream with rage. Many of them, they said, had been put in place by Napoleon. Yes, Napoleon. For example, you had to enter the school two by two, so if you got there alone, you had to wait outside for someone else who'd also come alone before you could enter. The rules we lived by were a million years old.

I felt like a condemned prisoner every morning and cried in my room every day after school. This was the worst. I would never be happy again.

January 23, 1965

HAPPINESS

CONS
1. *I hate my new school.*
2. ~~*My parents don't understand my situation.*~~
3. *I have no social life.*
4. *I have nobody with whom to discuss things with.*

PROS
a. The girls at school are nice.
b. I have less hours of math than at the other school.

Mum and I had been fighting a lot, but now that I was distraught about school, she was sympathetic, ready to listen and comfort me. She assured me that I should be patient; things would be fine.

I didn't believe her.

Within two weeks, I had my *blouse*, I got through the morning three-cheek kissing ritual as efficiently as the other girls — *Bonjour*, smack smack smack, thirty-eight times — and I spoke French. It felt like suitcases snapping open, one after the other, as I understood verbs, tenses, nouns. *Je ne peux pas parler français*, I learned to say, and then, *Je parle un peu mieux maintenant.* I speak better now. To make friends, I needed to learn to speak fluent French, and so I did.

By the end of my second week, I was able to tell a group of girls in the cloakroom that the French word for seal, *phoque*, sounded the same as a very bad word in English. "*Un très mauvais mot*," I said and waggled my finger, no no no. It felt like at last I could be myself again, even in another language. They giggled and covered their mouths with their hands. From then on, I was greeted in the morning with, "*Bonjour, Elisabet.*" Kiss kiss kiss. "*Phoque!*"

Jan. 30

My dear Ladies College Klassmates:
   ... I'm at a 100% French school so I speak French all day. I say the same idiotic things I said back home, but in French, which makes them much worse.
   The top foreign hit parade songs here are:

#*1. I feel fine* — Beatles.
#*2. It's all over now - ?*
#*3. Slow down* — Beatles.
#*4. I should have known better* — Beatles.
#*5. Time is on my side* — R. Stones.
#*6. She's a woman* — Beatles.

*What's IN there? Here — short, short hair, lace nylons,
tee shirts, check blouses, sloppy corduroy slacks with wide
bottoms, bright, loud check knee socks — knee socks are IN —
tiny little shoulder bags in a quilted material, long high boots,
suede suits, simple princess line sleeveless dresses with little
collars, sweaters with lace sleeves and collar, and turtlenecks,
as tight as possible — I have two, and boy! Are they sexy!
Imagine how they'd look on Nancy!*

In the lycée classrooms, I found out that any kind of imagi-
nation, discussion or creativity were no-no's. Teaching and
learning meant memorization; all you had to do for homework
was memorize every single fact in every textbook. Music class
had nothing to do with music, though there was an old record
player, and we did listen to some repetitive music by some ancient
guy called Lully. But mostly we were required to memorize the
dates of composers. "*Jean-Baptiste Lully,*" we intoned. "*Seize
cent trente-deux à seize cent quatre-vingt sept.*" 1632 to 1687.
That was music class.

Monsieur Paul McCartney, I wanted to chant, French style.
Dix-neuf cent quarante-deux à toujours. Because unlike boring
old Lully, Paul had talent and would live forever.

To find out who was working and who not, the teachers would
pick a student at random to go up to the front of the room, stand
on a little box and have questions thrown at her. If she didn't

know the answers, she'd humiliate herself in front of everyone and be given a *mauvaise note*. The first time I was called up to the little box, the teacher turned her back to me for a moment, and I opened my eyes wide, chattered my teeth and wobbled my knees, pretending to be terrified. They all gasped. The teacher whipped around, and I smiled warmly at her. At lunch, the girls told me I was *courageuse*. Brave — me!

Dealing with the quizzes was simple; if I didn't know the answer, I pretended I couldn't understand the question.

"Je m'excuse, madame, mais je ne comprends pas."

Best of all was English class. I had to take English along with everyone else, and at the beginning, it was ridiculously hard to look at my own language from a distance. What tense was "given"? How do you spell "brought"? On our first English test, to everyone's delight except mine, I came second. First was Véronique, whom I called Mushroom Girl, a scrawny teacher's pet with bags under her eyes and pale grey skin who memorized everything, even the dates of obscure composers we weren't studying.

I copied some of my schoolmates' homework answers to send to my friends back home: *One year ago than I lesson to the Englisch*, wrote Chantal. *The man was smashed on the glound, his eye was shutt*, wrote Antoinette. *He was dead or didding.*

One snowy day, Madeleine pointed to the sky and said proudly, "Eet ees renninge." How I enjoyed listening to those crazy girls.

We read short stories and then did vocabulary. After one story by Katherine Mansfield, an old-fashioned writer I'd never heard of, the English teacher brought up the word *valise*, which meant "suitcase."

"In dees story," she said, "we 'ave learn dat de eengleesh for *valise* ees 'dress basket.' *Valise*," she repeated, "dress basket." I almost didn't correct her, with a vision of all these girls landing in London and asking the porter to help carry their dress basket. Finally, I did point out that this was no longer the right word, that the word now, the girls chanted after me, was "zoot kes." The English teacher didn't mind me speaking up, luckily, but the other teachers did. I spoke up anyway and got my share of *mauvaises notes*.

But I was going to get out of there; my classmates weren't. All that mattered to them was underlining everything in the right colours — red, green and blue. We spent hours with our little rulers, underlining in different colours, using special clicky pens that had all three colours inside.

Mon dieu. Exciting.

One day there was much buzzing in the schoolyard, and I was told that another *Americaine* had started at the school in *troisième*, the grade above me. A group took me to meet her and stood, fascinated, watching the encounter. She had shoulder-length scraggly white-blonde hair and glasses, was wearing penny loafers — so American — and was the most wretched-looking girl I had ever seen. At least she wouldn't have to endure the unique Rosie welcome; she was already wearing her *blouse*. I had obviously been pointed out to her too.

"Hi," I said. No cheek kisses for us. "My name's Beth." What pleasure to speak my own language.

"I hate this place," she replied. "I hate everything about it. How can you stand it? It's like jail, they scream at you and the girls are nasty."

"It's not so bad," I said. "I guess I'm used to it. The lunches are really good. Anyway, hey, good luck."

I went back to my classmates, and we never spoke again. I didn't even find out her name. She was in a black hole, and I didn't want to be down there with her. Chantal told me that in January, when I'd first walked in, everyone in my class was prepared to envy or even hate *l'Americaine*, but not simply to like her. Luckily, I didn't know that.

As the weeks went by, I made friends — Marie-Josée, Marie-France, Marie-Christine — but no close friends. I was always an outsider, not once invited to someone's house or to a social event. The girls had their own cliques and didn't open them to foreigners, no matter how many funny bad words they were taught. When our school pictures came back, Louise told me her father had asked her to point out my face. I was in the back row.

"*Ah — un vrai geule americain*," he'd said. A real American mug.

"*Mais non, c'est un vrai geule canadien!*" I protested, for the first and only time.

The one class with a little bit of creativity was art class, where I had no talent at all. One night as I tried to finish my homework, a watercolour of the *SS France*, Mum saw my splashes and offered to help. She took the paper, dipped the brush in the watercolours and, eyes sparkling, painted away. Presto, out came a stunning boat, with golden lights in the portholes and smoke floating from the stack. At school, the teacher looked at my paper with amazement.

"*Tu l'as fait toi-même?*" she asked.

"*Mais oui, madame, bien sûr je l'ai fait,*" I said indignantly; of course I did it myself! I got 19 out of 20 for my ocean liner. But looking at it made me uncomfortable. I remembered the time at home when Mum came running into my room to tell me that the Nova Scotia Flower Show was coming up, and there was a new Wildflower Arranging Competition for Children Under Twelve. I should enter, she said. What was she talking about? I had no interest in wildflowers. Mum took me to Callaghan's field, the empty lot at the back of our yard, and picked a bunch of wildflowers, telling me what they were — "Queen Anne's lace, yarrow, comfrey..." She put them in a pot she'd made herself at pottery class, entered it in the competition, and I won First Prize in the Nova Scotia Wildflower Arranging Competition for Children Under Twelve — a blue ribbon and ten silver dollars. Receiving those heavy coins didn't make me feel good though.

Mum was keen to help with my next school art project, but I said no thanks and painted a tree in winter without assistance. I tried to create dark Canadian branches laden with snow, but the result was the usual scribble. I got 12. And that was okay.

MY MOTHER WAS taking French classes at the Alliance Française, so her French was improving, but she hadn't made any friends and needed someone to talk to. Luckily for her, she had me.

I wondered why at home she had so few girlfriends. There was only one, really, Dottie, our paediatrician's receptionist, a plump, motherly woman. Mum usually disliked women who worked, but she liked Dottie, who was, naturally, British. I once heard them discussing the book *The Feminine Mystique* by Betty Friedan. Lots of women in magazines and newspapers had been talking about this book as if it was important, so I was curious to know what my mother thought. "I took one look at the picture of Betty Friedan," she said to Dottie, "and I put the book down."

Betty Friedan was not a glamourpuss, but that didn't seem to me to be a good reason not to read an important book. But then, my mother only read lying down, and as soon as she lay down with a book, she fell asleep. "I don't know how you have time to sit around like that," she often said, nagging me to do some chore when I wanted to finish the chapter. "There's so much to do." Do. That meant folding laundry, drying dishes, picking the pits out of a bubbling pot of Damson plums before she made her jam.

Though truthfully, the jam was delicious, and I didn't have to do much more than that. Mum did it all.

It wasn't her fault that she didn't work. In 1940, my mother had quit her grammar school, where she was a top student on a scholarship, to help the British war effort. She'd joined the Land Army, milking cows on a farm, and then the secret team at Bletchley Park, helping to decode German submarine messages, which sounded like the most spine-tingling job. But "Leaving school was the worst mistake of my life," she always said, when telling this story. "Never interrupt your schooling, Beth. See where it left me — high and dry."

Well — it left you with a nice house and a nice family, I wanted to say. Is that high and dry? But I knew what she meant. Unlike the women scientists Dad worked with, she didn't have training or a university education or even a high school diploma. Yes, when we lived in London, she'd taken courses in social work from the London School of Economics, and when we got back from England, she found a job as an apprentice social worker. Her first client was a woman with two young children whose husband beat her.

"Her story was so terrible," she told me, "I felt so sorry for her that I burst into tears and had to run to the bathroom to cry. I was a ghastly mess." She never went back.

Almost none of the Halifax mothers we knew had jobs either, except looking after their families. The men were out making a living, and the women were at home, sewing clothes and making nice things to eat, always there when we kids got home from school. Almost every woman we knew was married with kids, except for Marie and Jean, both single women who lived alone and had jobs. They weren't either of them pretty; probably couldn't find a man to marry them. I did not know of one person who was divorced.

My mother had no admiration or respect for the female scientists Daddy knew. In fact, she really disliked those women. She would tell me how unhappy their husbands and children were; how working women, because they were off selfishly pursuing their own careers and goals, had to rely on maids without education to raise their kids and get meals on the table — unhealthy meals too. I was grateful Mum was at home taking care of us and not selfishly pursuing her own goals, whatever those might be.

But still, I wanted to keep my lonely mother at a distance.

The trouble was, I was lonely too; Mum was all I had, and we were getting closer. She asked my advice on what to wear and do and all kinds of things; she listened; she was fun. My mother had always liked to confide in me and for me to confide in her, heart to heart and woman to woman, even when I was quite small. But never more so than here. I got used to her teary visits to my room.

She came in one day, clutching her constant companion, a shred of Kleenex, to tell me that Dad's Polish lab assistant at home, Jadwiga, wanted to come work with him at his lab in Paris. "Your father's all for it," she hissed. Jadwiga, Mum said, did all Dad's work for him, which was why he liked her so much. I'd met dumpy Jadwiga when I went to visit Dad's sour-smelling lab in the basement of the Forrest Building at Dal. Just like the mad scientists in the movies, my father wore a white lab coat and hovered over rows of bubbling test tubes.

"I'm convinced," Mum said, blowing her nose, "that your father and Jadwiga are having an affair."

"What? That's ridiculous," I said, shocked. Utterly impossible! "Jadwiga's chunky and has bleached blonde hair with dark roots showing. Dad wouldn't be interested in someone so cheap-looking. Anyway, she wouldn't do that, Mum. She's nice."

No she was not nice, Mum was having none of it. "If he brings her over here," she said, "I've told him I'm leaving. I'll take you with me and go to London."

My heart turned over. Her words brought back a time I did not want to think about — our last sabbatical, when our family nearly split apart forever. Now she was talking about leaving and taking me with her, again.

"Your father has absolutely no respect for the institution of marriage," she went on. "To him, it's just a scientific joining for the purpose of sexual satisfaction and procreation."

What was she talking about? I'd always been proud that my mother would never have the opportunity to be jealous. Men falling in love with their secretaries and having suspicious wives,

I thought — that happens in comic strips or to weak men who work in offices, not brilliant professors in labs.

Mum telling me secrets about Dad made me feel grown-up and special but also angrier at him. As if I should reject him not just for what he did to me but for what he did to her. Though that was harder to see.

I had to get her mind off of this.

"Mum, don't be silly and stop driving yourself nuts," I said. "Come on, let's go watch TV. It's almost time for *Monsieur Ed.*"

I walked out of my room, and she followed. But she'd be back. *The older I get*, I wrote later, *the more she tells me ... and the less I tell her. Funny.*

But that was wishful thinking, really. I told her a lot. Everything. It's just that so far, there wasn't much to tell.

DAD HAD ACTUALLY rented a television set. He didn't mind us watching here because it helped our French, though by now we all spoke pretty well. Enjoying French television, which had lots of dull talky shows and no advertising at all, was one of our fun times. We liked best the re-runs of American shows dubbed into French — *Bonanza, I Love Lucy, The Untouchables. Mr. Ed* became *Monsieur Ed.* The three of us laughed to see Monsieur Ed the horse move his lips up and down and speak in French. Instead of "Aw, come on, Wilbur," he drawled, "*Voyons, Weelburr.*"

It was good to hear my mother laugh. I kept reminding myself that I should be more sympathetic to her. Mum said she had a bad heart; we heard a lot about her heart. She'd spent time as a child in bed with many illnesses, maybe because she grew so tall so fast, and when she contracted rheumatic fever, her heart, she said, was damaged. Because of that, as an adult, she had to lie down most afternoons and take a nap. But beforehand, before she did anything, she had to have a cup of tea.

"I'm feeling dreadful," she'd say, from her position on the sofa. "How lovely it would be to have a cup of tea."

Or: "Perhaps I should get up now and go make myself a cup of tea."

Or: "Beth, how would YOU like a nice cup of tea?"

They all worked. Her tea appeared.

Guiltily, I had doubts about my mother's bad heart. When there was something she really wanted to do, she had more energy than anyone alive. Visiting art galleries, gardening or buying gigantic shoes at Tall Girls in New York, Mum was unstoppable. With a tennis racquet in her hand, she was petrifying. The rest of the time, she liked to drift gently onto the nearest sofa and hope for a cup of tea.

Feb. 9

Yesterday, you've no idea how hopeless and dreary I felt. This evening I refused to let Mum do the dishes, so Dave and I did them, and after a bit, I felt better, because I was doing something for someone else, and not thinking of myself! I've also formed an opinion about my sad feelings — the last ones, and the latest ones, were in the region of the time when I have my period. I expect it shortly. Maybe it's that.

Mum and I have never been so close — I love her so! You've no idea how many sacrifices she makes for us, and how much she works. And she's a wonderful, sweet, gentle woman, and I here-by take back anything mean, insulting and petty I've said about her on these hallowed pages. When we go back to a more normal situation, fighting etc., then I'll complain again. Now, I adore her.

That weekend, I wrote an angry story. Paul had found out I was secretly taking art classes with a man friend. He came to the mad conclusion that I was having an affair and rushed home in a fury to confront me.

"You're just jealous!" I shouted.

His breath was coming fast, but besides anger there was pain on his face. I know he hates these sort of scenes.

"Of course I am!" he said. "I did marry you, even if it was in ignorance, and I don't want my wife to become a whore!"

"Well!" I snarled. "You bastard! Now I see how much faith you have in me! You jealous son-of-a-bitch! I wanted these classes to be a surprise to you!"

"You mean you wanted to keep your underhand dealings a secret, like a coward." He took a deep breath. "If you want a ... a divorce, you can have one!"

This took me by surprise. Suddenly my knees crumpled, and I sat down and cried. Paul, with a white face, sat down too.

"I ... I only wanted to get a di ... diploma and surprise you," I sobbed. "I thought you'd be pleased! The man was only a ... a friend." I lifted my head to look at him. "I've ... never done anything with him, Paul. Really."

Before I knew it, there was an arm around my waist and a soft hand on my forehead, pushing the hair out of my eyes.

"There, there," he said in a trembling voice. I turned to him and held him tight, tight to me, feeling his heart beating and the slight tremor of his hands as he stroked my hair. He got out his handkerchief and wiped my eyes. When he spoke, his voice was thick and pleading.

"Beth, I'm … I'm sorry."
"Oh Paul," clutching him. "I love you so."
*Since that fight we have loved each other more than
ever, for I found in Paul a gentle, forgiving side and also a
manly protecting side.*
*And he found, inside the outside me, a little me that
needs protecting.*

There was a time when Paul and I would never have had even
a momentary disagreement. That's marriage for you, I thought.
Like my parents — when they weren't busy fighting for world
peace, they were busy fighting each other.

RINGO GOT MARRIED! My Halifax friends and I were excited
— especially when we did the math and figured out how many
months early his and Maureen's baby was going to be born. Oh
those naughty Beatles. It reminded me of a favourite joke of
ours at school:

Why did the elephant marry the mouse?
Had to.

I didn't even try to translate the joke into French for my
friends. But for Lea, I did a laborious translation of an article on
the Beatles in the new teen magazine *Mademoiselle Age Tendre*.
Paul doesn't cease to make publicity about the Beatles, I wrote
in tiny writing on thin blue airmail paper, proud that my French
was now this good.

*Of the four lads with hair on the neck and the mop like a
stack of hay, of the identical clothes and the continental
cut, of the contagious attitude, Paul makes himself much*

anxiety because the people think that the Beatles are inapproachable types who live in a tower of ivory which they leave only if one throws money while telling them to sing. The phenomenal success which he shares with his three friends leaves Paul speechless yet. "I never dreamed that someone could make a discovery of me or anything of that sort. To be a discovery is a thing which one sees in books."

Today when he reads of that in books, it is himself who is in question. Occasionally, he really wishes that he reads of someone else.

I myself did not wish to read of someone else.

12

March

Something bad WAS happening to my father. When I got in from the lycée one day, Dad was already home from work. He was furious, talking in a loud voice on the phone — it sounded as though to someone in Halifax. We never called long distance except in emergencies; it was too expensive. Was this Jadwiga? Was that actually happening? My gut convulsed. But no one said anything, so I didn't either.

The next day, another long-distance call, and after he'd hung up, he said some bad words and went out, banging the door. Then silence for days, then yelling into the phone again.

"Nothing to be done, the sons of bitches," he said to Mum, who of course was leaking tears. When she and I were alone, I finally asked what was going on.

"It's terrible, Beth," she said. "Your father has been at Dal fourteen years and was next in line to be head of his department, but he found out last week they've hired Don Schmidt instead."

I remembered Don Schmidt from dinners at our house. Small, puffy, pompous.

"I don't get it," I said. "If Dad's next in line, then he has to get the job, doesn't he?"

My mother tore at the salad spinner. "His boss Millard waited till your father was safely in France and then suddenly retired. Dad wasn't consulted or even told. Millard's boss the dean is afraid of Dad and didn't want him to be head. Your father is shattered. Both Millard and Don are good friends of his. Were."

Poor Daddy! I felt terrible for him. It wasn't his fault; he worked so hard, he was a great man who did a lot for the world and deserved much better. It amazed me that it didn't matter how old you were, there was still some idiot bossing you around and letting you down. I didn't think my mother was being sympathetic enough. Dad needed kindness. He needed a friend. When he came home from the lab and stood pouring a whiskey in the kitchen, I went in and said, "Daddy, Mum told me what happened in the department. I think it's really unfair."

"Me too," he said. "I think so too." He took a long drink. "To succeed in life, Pupikina," he said, "you have to be a hypocrite, and I'm not good at that."

"You certainly aren't," I said, wanting to cry, and he looked down at me. And then he put his arm around my shoulders and gave me a squeeze.

Maybe for other girls, it was normal, that sort of thing.

THERE WAS A photograph in an album at home, one of my favourites, taken in September 1951 when Dad was recovering from polio. In the photo, my father is standing inside a metal walker. At thirteen months old, I am holding onto the back of my stroller, beside him. We are both trying to swing our stubborn legs forward.

My father and I learned to walk together. That bond lived in my bones.

DADDY WENT ON shouting into the phone, but the battle was over, and he had lost. He looked depressed for a day or two but immediately started to make calls about another job. He was going to quit Dalhousie and go somewhere else. I didn't want to leave Halifax — I loved our town and just wanted to go home — but this time, I agreed with him. He'd been treated badly, maybe by the anti-Semitism he sometimes suspected, and so we'd have to leave. I heard them talk about a possible opening for him in the States somewhere, but then that vanished too.

"Your father has ruined his chances with Rochester," Mum came in to tell me, bitterly. "It's as if he does it deliberately. They asked about his politics, he went on about the Vietnam War, and that was that. I understand how he feels — I'm against the war too — but he needs a job!"

I'd only heard of the Vietnam War because some people had stood outside the gates of my school, handing out leaflets that looked like nasty anti-American propaganda to me. I didn't want us to go hungry. What was wrong with that man?

Mum said we didn't have enough money to last the year in France because Dad was so bad at managing money. She asked if I would speak to him about our budget, because he didn't hear her when she spoke. "He needs to be sensible, after all," she said. "Much as he'd like to forget it, he has a family to support."

"You think he'll hear ME?" I asked. "Me of all people?"

But she really wanted me to, so when he came in hugging a bottle of wine, I asked, "What about our budget, Dad? How will we last the year when you buy wine like that?"

"Mind your own bloody business!" he shouted. But I wasn't sorry I'd spoken. Mum needed my help to deal with him. He had to be sensible, after all. She'd said so, and I believed her.

My comfort came from knowing that one day, I would survive without my parents. I'd grow up and get married and leave them behind. Soon. And yet the thought of living without them petrified me.

DESPITE THE STACKS of memorization and the incomprehensible geometry and algebra homework — if even my dad couldn't figure it out, how could a lunkhead like me? — I was managing to make teen time for myself in the evenings. Hélène had been replaced with gear Radio Luxembourg, broadcasting from a pirate barge in the Channel somewhere. Often the sound coming from my little transistor was frustratingly blurry, but when it wasn't, I went to bed with music tucked under my ear. There were new Beatles songs, all the best, especially Paul's haunting "I'll Follow the Sun" and "She's a Woman." Yes, Paul, I cried, I'm a woman who understands, I'm a woman who loves her man.

Why didn't he hear me?

Though I did think, the first time I heard the lines, "My love don't give me presents. I know that she's no peasant," that they were not the best Beatle lyrics I'd ever heard. It was okay to be a bit critical occasionally, to show I wasn't a complete pushover. There was so little to criticize.

I listened to the Stones, the Kinks, the Seekers, the Hollies, the Animals, Herman's Hermits — very cute — and Petula Clark's smash hit "Downtown"; she was popular in France because she was married to a Frenchman and spoke French with a sweet British accent. I liked P. J. Proby and cool Dusty Springfield and her "Wishin' and Hopin'." Handsome Cliff Richard and the Shadows.

Unfortunately, they also played the Dave Clark Five. My stupid brother, who knew how much I hated them, liked to chant their songs at the top of his voice — "BITS AND PIECES!" — and told me once that Paul looked like Dave Clark. I could have murdered him. My disdain for those copycat drips had not diminished one bit. *I wish*, I wrote to Hilly, *that they would become instinct*!

And the same for Jane Asher, who never stopped doing horrible things to Paul. And to me. In one story, sloshed and slurring her words, she telephoned me on the eve of my wedding to Paul to tell me she was pregnant with Paul's baby. The nerve! I slapped Paul across the face, walked out and called off the wedding. Though Paul protested his innocence, I would not relent.

When they found out what was going on, the other Beatles
called a meeting.

"Well, Paul," said John, with mock severity. "You've
ruined us."

Paul flushed.

George said admiringly, "We all underestimated you.
Innocent Paul."

"Whenever we went marauding, you always stayed
behind," said John. "Why? Did you think Jane was better
than those girls down at the Cozy Dancing Salon?"

Paul exploded. "Look, I did not touch Jane in the way
you think. Blimey, I've petted. So has everybody, like!"

"Yes," replied John, in a true serious tone. "But Paul,
you were already engaged. What's the matter with Beth?"

"Nothing. She's fine. I wasn't engaged when I ... when
Jane and I ... oh, you know what I mean."

Cynthia Lennon rushed to the rescue. She wormed her way
into Jane Asher's drunken confidence and got her to confess about
the affair. The father of this vile alcoholic's baby was actually ...
Dave Clark!

Natch.

The only hatred I'd ever felt as strong as the one I had for Jane
was for Brenda, my enemy at Tower Road, who had done her
best to mock and exclude me. Maybe, I thought, it was blondes
I hated. But no — my dear Lea was blonde. Just bitchy blondes.
And then I found out Jane Asher was not blonde; she was a red-
head! How like her.

It was a point of pride that I did not like any American music,
no greaser Elvis Pretzel or squeaky Beach Boys, except Roy
Orbison's "Pretty Woman," the best of the best. Otherwise, only
British groups for me. But my school friends got me reading

Mademoiselle Age Tendre and *Salut les Copains*, the French teen magazines, and learning about the French pop stars — Johnny Hallyday, Sylvie Vartan, Sheila, Claude François and especially lovely Françoise Hardy with the perfect long straight hair we all coveted, who maybe, one article said with illustrations, set her hair with giant rollers on top and scotch-taped her bangs. I almost fitted in when I could discuss not just Paul but soulful Françoise and the other *yéyé* singers with my friends at school. I even bought one of Françoise's EPs and Johnny Hallyday singing the Animals' "House of the Rising Sun" in French. The French mags had lots of stuff on British pop stars like Marianne Faithfull. And important articles, like "What kind of breasts do you have?" Mine, I mourned to read, were the ones called *boutons* — *les plus petits*. *Boutons* was the French word for pimples. If they don't grow, it said, see a doctor.

Helpful.

I read that Paul's father had remarried. What was that like for my boy? I decided he would be happy for his dad on the surface and very sweet to the newly-weds, but secretly heartbroken. Because to him, the sacred memory of his beloved mother must never be disturbed.

THERE WAS TIME in the evenings and on the weekends to write to Babs, Hillary and Lea and in my diary, and especially to explore the sweet dailyness of love. Inspired by the tragic lovers in the movie *West Side Story* that Dad had recently taken us to see, I imagined that my dear fiancé Paul and I had been forced apart by my cruel parents, and I wrote him a wistful letter. *They wanted me to fall in love with Albert Einstein or Yehudi Menuin*, I told him. *They don't think one knows one's mind at eighteen — I do! I love you.*

To go with it, I traced a picture from a magazine of two lovers kissing, adding my own touches, the girl with long straight Françoise Hardy hair, an ID bracelet that said, "Paul," and tears of farewell, and the boy an ID bracelet that said, "BK."

Moi.

Our lives in Paris were routine now — school for me and David, who was doing really well at the local elementary school; research at the Institut Pasteur for Dad; and, great news for us all, Cordon Bleu cooking classes for Mum. She went to the local market on Saturday mornings and came back with food so delicious I could not get enough. The bread called *brioche*, round, sweet and warm, with a giant chunk of fresh paté — I had never tasted anything with such flavour. *Oeufs mayonnaise*

— hard-boiled eggs smeared with freshly made thick yellow mayonnaise. Vache Qui Rit, little triangles of cheese, sharp and smooth. So good, each bite a revelation in my mouth. I'd always been slender, so my little potbelly was something new, and I liked it; maybe it would help me get some curves. Before, my only concern was trying to choke down enough so I wouldn't get yelled at. It was different here, with food tasting so good.

Daddy had always nagged me to eat, but now, as I cut myself another thick slice of sunny brioche and smeared it with paté, he started nagging me to stop.

"That's enough," he commanded, to my surprise. "You're filling out. No more."

That was something I'd not heard before. Filling out? I had never once thought about the size of my body or my weight, about whether it was good to be skinny or medium-sized or fat, only about the bumps on my chest. How much, in fact, did I weigh? I had absolutely no idea.

And I did not care. I did not care.

What I had to say to Dad was: Phooey. What did it matter if you filled out as long as you were healthy, and food, for the first time, tasted great?

April 13

I've been thinking — why do I, E. Kaplan, have the right to be unhappy? Here I am, well off, with an easy life, comfortable and sure, in Paris, going to movies, buying clothes etc. etc. I don't have the right to be unhappy, to get those feelings, to be selfish. I'm spoiled, spoiled, spoiled. Here I am in Paris, having new experiences every day, and what do I write about? My unhappiness, my selfish feelings — God, I'm self-centred, selfish and horrible. REPENT!!

It gave me pleasure now to think and even dream in French, and to read French books not just for school but for pleasure. We went regularly to see French movies, though Dad wouldn't take us to the film I really wanted to see — *Goldfinger*, with handsome sexy Double Agent 007, James Bond.

April 14

An amazing peace has fallen over my soul. I feel happy, well-adjusted, normal ... no more "feelings" etc. How nice, for a change.

There was another family melodrama. Mum decided that since she couldn't find any clothes in petite France for a woman her height, she'd have a suit made, and because she could never have made up her mind alone, she got Dad to come buy material with her. Hallelujah, I thought, peace and quiet, my parents off on an errand together. But Mum soon stormed back in a complete state, and Dad walked in behind her, went straight into the little toilet room and slammed the door. He'd brought his serious French newspaper without any pictures in with him, so I knew he'd be there for some time.

"Your father is so impatient. He was no help at all!" my mother exclaimed, tossing a paper bag on the table. "He said he liked the very first material we saw, so though I wanted to look at all the others, we ended up getting that. It's terribly expensive and absolutely horrible. A disaster. Look!" And she showed me a tweedy material with lots of light blue and a bit of bright gold.

"Actually, Mum," I said, "it's nice."

"It's ghastly!" she said. "A terrible mistake."

She had the suit made anyway. It looked like the tweedy suits by the famous designer Chanel, but it wasn't until she'd had several compliments that she stopped blaming Dad and began to believe it looked okay on her. Sometimes I had to feel sorry for my dad.

But then he'd do something mean, like Mum complaining about a terrible pain, and he'd look at me with a grin. As if he was doubting her. She was so often ill, but that was not her fault. It was not fair to make fun of someone in such constant pain and distress.

Although her pain and distress were so constant, I did have to wonder sometimes myself if they were real. I wondered secretly. Guiltily. But wonder I did.

April 30

The world has changed lots, loads of people have died only I've forgotten who, everybody is more anti-American than before etc. etc. The family hasn't changed only everybody hates each other more than ever and Dad changes from nasty to sweet. Mum and I are very close and Dave is horrible.

As for me, the subject is so depressing, I don't even want to discuss it.

SO THINGS WITH Dad and me were the same, sometimes okay, mostly bad, him snarling a lot. One Saturday, I got dressed up to go out, wearing skin-tight stretch pants and a tight maroon poor-boy turtleneck, teasing my hair a little, putting on pink lipstick. Here in France, you had to make sure you looked good all the time, no shirking. My father looked up from his newspaper.

"Are you trying to look older?" he said. "It's not working. With your mentality, it's only twelve-year old boys who'll be interested."

What was I supposed to say? Why did he feel he had to insult me? I walked out and slammed the door behind me. Well, no, I wanted to slam the door, and I did make a bit of noise. But not a lot.

I WENT OUT to wander. To get away from our little place and the nutty people inside, I'd often take the metro, get off anywhere and just walk around, down crooked little streets, looking up at the narrow white-gold buildings with their intricate black balconies, trying to spy on the French lives inside. Or I'd discover a monument or a church to visit or an interesting store for window-shopping. One day I heard music, followed the sound and came to a square, a leafy green oasis hemmed in on all sides by tall houses. People were standing around a young man, who sat on a park bench in the centre, playing the guitar beautifully. In the open guitar case at his feet, instead of a request for money, was a handwritten notice: *Pas d'argent, s'il vous plaît. Ecoutez seulement.* No money, please. Just listen. So we did.

That was one of those moments that, even as it was happening, I locked up safely in my memory forever: the elegant square and graceful trees in the sun, the crowd gathered to hear the young man's fingers speed up and down, music spilling out under a canopy of green.

But that Saturday, as I was meandering down a hidden street, a man dashed up to me. He was olive-skinned with tangled black hair, a ragged flapping coat and whirling eyes.

"*Mademoiselle*," he said urgently. I didn't know what to do. I was scared but didn't want to be rude.

"*Oui, monsieur?*" I said.

He peered at me. "*Avez-vous faites l'amour ... avec un homme?*"

"*Non, monsieur,*" I squeaked, scurrying away. No, I had not made love with a man, what a disturbing question. Was he following me? Should I scream? Only when I'd emerged into a busy street did I turn around. He was gone.

My carefree wandering stopped. I stayed close to main streets after that, when I wandered at all. But then I was stuck, because staying home was a complete drag.

A FEW WEEKS later, when supper was late and I was very hungry, I walked into the kitchen. Mum was ironing, Dad frying some steak. They commanded me to set the table. Mum said, "Are you cold? You looked cold when you came in."

I was always cold. Dad called me *frileuse*, which means "always cold."

"Yes, I'm freezing." I let out a big sigh. "And I feel faint from hunger."

That brought the wave over my head.

"I'm tempted to smack her so hard when she's acting the drama queen like that," said my father.

I walked into the living room to set the table, as the voices trailed after me. "You know, Gord," said my mother, "if that child were left to fend for herself, she'd starve to death. She'd live on tea and toast."

Dad saying, "No university will ever accept her, with work habits like hers…"

I went to my room to avoid hearing them, clenching my hands, biting my tongue, murmuring, "Paul, Paul, Paul." If I didn't have Paul to love me, I thought, I'd go insane.

When supper began, so did Dad, talking to Mum as if I weren't there.

"That child really should get an award for melodrama, the Sarah Heartburn Oscar."

I hung onto my dear dream husband. But though I fought to hold them back, the tears started.

"I don't want to hear that noise any more," Dad said. "You can cry all you want, but from now on, I do not want to hear it."

I fled to my room, locked the door behind me and wept without making a sound. At least I had this haven, this plain room with my fifty Beatle pictures and my diary. After dinner, Dad wanted to talk to me and tried to get in. When he discovered the locked door, he was furious.

"This door is not under any circumstances to be locked again. Do you hear me?" he shouted.

If only he would disappear. Vanish forever. I could not have hated him more.

I SPENT THE weekend shut in my room with a luscious new story I described to Hilly as a "three-nighter," meaning I could spin out the excitement that long. Paul, my husband, landed in hospital, desperately ill with pneumonia. I was frantic with worry. One night the doctor called to tell me to come immediately; Paul was dying. I sped to the hospital in Paul's Aston-Martin and ran to his side. There he lay, struggling to breathe under an oxygen tent, looking small and helpless, his eyelashes dark against his white, white face.

> ... The doctor pulled Paul's left hand out of the oxygen tent and took his pulse. "Very weak," he said. "I'd give him two hours." My heart became cold as ice.
>
> "Doctor?" I said. "Could I ... could I hold his hand?"
> He looked uncertain, then decided. "O.K."
> I reached into the oxygen tent and took Paul's hand, so cold where it had once been so warm, so tender. I held it as if it were my last possession on earth. It almost was.
> Maybe this is my imagination, but I think that helped him. When the pain was bad, he would try to clench his

hand, but only succeeded in grasping mine. After a few
hours, hours that I lived in mortal fear, as the doctor had
only given him two of them, I noticed that his breathing
seemed slightly easier. I called in the doctor, who wasn't
impressed, only concerned about me.

"You've been here almost 20 hours already. Do go
home and get some sleep."

"Sleep? Are you crazy? I'm sure he's getting better,
doctor! I'm sure!"

He looked pityingly at me, went out and brought some
coffee. I almost spilled it, as I drank with my left hand. My
right was in Paul's and I wasn't letting go!

Hours more I sat there, and I became certain that his
pain had become less and his breathing easier. Heart full
of hope, I continued my watch, though my lids were heavy.
John entered. "Do you realize," he whispered, " that it's
one o'clock and you have been here twenty-four hours? Do
get some sleep!"

"Oh, John," excitedly, "I'm sure he's getting better!"

He stayed with me for two hours; we were joined by
Cynthia and George for a bit. They were all as hopeful as I.

Gradually Paul seemed to work his way out of the
death cloud that shadowed him. Even the doctor was
encouraged.

"It's a miracle, Mrs. McCartney!" he said.

I didn't know who to thank — God, or the penisillan.

I spent days drifting inside the story. I could see him in that
hospital bed, thin and pale; I could feel my hand reaching for
his and the warmth that moved between us and saved his life.
My heart felt swollen, twice its normal size with love and
happiness.

May 14

I've been reading over this diary and I figure that I've said some pretty sensible things and some pretty stupid things as well. Maybe I should seriously consider becoming a writer.

What could be better than writing? Only love.

ONE EARLY EVENING, after school, I got off the metro and walked toward the ugly concrete apartment building in the distance — our home. A cloudy grey day, and around me, the dumpy buildings of Gentilly. I was wearing my favourite outfit, a green corduroy A-line skirt and light green poor-boy sweater, carrying my heavy *cartable* — bookbag — full of homework. Instead of passing the *boulangerie*, a bakery with a window filled with sticky golden treasure, I went in.

"*Bonne après-midi monsieurdame*," sang the little woman with the moustache who ran the place. I loved how customers always greeted the people serving in stores, and how shopkeepers called everyone *monsieurdame*, as if they couldn't tell what sex you were.

"*Bonne après-midi, madame, un pain au chocolat s'il vous plaît*," I replied. She handed me a little paper bag.

I resumed my walk home, taking a careful bite of the flaky pastry surrounding a dark river of chocolate. Suddenly, I had another of those moments when the camera flashed, freezing the instant forever in a mental photograph album. I was walking on the sidewalk beside the dirty cobblestone street of Gentilly, my left shoulder weighed down with my *cartable*, and in my right hand, the delicious treat. I had taken two bites. How many were left? Three or four, depending on how *pressée* I was.

I bit, chewed, looked at what was left. Time was passing this way. Just as my *pain au chocolat* was disappearing, so was my life.

I tried to slow down.

Another bite — the sweet stretchy crumbiness of the pastry, the explosion of dark sweet melting that was the chocolate. I explored it in my mouth as I walked. Soon I would be home. Soon my treat would be gone. Soon I would be old.

Only two bites left — a small piece. I held it, felt it in my fingers, brought it to my nose and inhaled deeply. The yeasty smell of France. If I didn't eat this piece but kept it safely somewhere, would that mean I could control time? That I would not die? But I couldn't stop, it was too good, and I was still hungry. I took the second last bite. Across the street, a fat old woman of maybe fifty opened her door and came out with her plaid shopping cart. She wore a shapeless yellow tweed coat and clumpy brown shoes and was frowning at the sky. I promised myself that no matter how old I got, I would never look like that.

This was it — the last bite. I popped it into my mouth, swallowed, and licked my fingers. The *pain au chocolat* was gone. It had been there, a puff of deliciousness in my hand, and now my hand was empty. I felt my body moving home, young in her green clothes.

Here I am.

I am here.

13

May

There was a rumour that the Beatles would be coming to Paris; I scanned the papers every day for news. I'd be in the front row with a sophisticated smile on my face, so gorgeous, Paul would look down and ...

No. All he'd see would be a messy, hoarse, screaming speck in the 89th row. Sob.

I heard it on the radio first — *the most glorious, fabulous, marvellous, gear, terrific, super, fantabulous, stupendous, splendifourous news*, I wrote to Hilly — the Beatles *were* coming to Paris, to do two shows on the same day. Two shows on the same day! I flipped — all my dreams had come true. No, I thought, better not hope too much, something would come to spoil it. I'd get smallpox or bubonic plague, or my parents would refuse to let me go. No, nothing could spoil that day. If they said I couldn't go, I'd run away from home.

"Fuck 'em," I thought, "if they can't take a joke."

They said if I did all my homework every night till the end of school, I could go. Yes yes cross my heart and hope to die. I gathered all my savings and flew to the Palais des Sports box office, a dark little opening with brass bars that was the window to paradise. There was no one else in line. I didn't want to be greedy; the best seats were thirty francs — expensive, six dollars — but there were ones at twenty francs and at ten. For the afternoon show, I bought the best seat they had, in the eighth row centre. For the evening, I only allowed myself a ten franc seat — two dollars; on the side but still close. The tickets glowed in my purse on the metro home. I was sure everyone could see that light beaming out.

Waiting was murder, but to pass the time, I wrote lots of letters home, telling them about the upcoming concert. It was mean but also hard to resist — how lucky was I to have this incredible piece of good fortune? June 20th. How to wait that long?

In a British magazine, the interviewer was with the Beatles during a meal. "I'm sorry to interrupt you while you're eating," he said, "but what do you think you'll be doing in five years?"

"Still eating," said John.

June 6

I'm still afraid there are two things that can stop me from going — Death and other tragedies like stomach flu (I'd go even so) or a broken leg (ditto) or ... my Father, much more formidable.

Paul has become a complete angel in my eyes — he isn't human any more. I've lost my virginity to him about twenty times, and go over and over our nights together. I have lots of excess affection, and I've got to get it out of my system somehow!

I wrote about Paul teaching me to make love. It was hard to write, because it was about something I wanted and did not want, something that frightened me and interested me very much.

182

Paul looked at me. "Should we?" he said.

I clasped my clammy hands nervously and looked at him. "I ... I suppose so."

"Do you want to?" he smiled.

"No!" I replied.

"Well then, let's not."

"But Paul ..." I blushed, red and stammering.

He decided to be blunt. "Are you a virgin?"

Heart pounding, I replied in a whisper, "Yes." Then, gathering courage, "Are you?"

A small smile turned up the corners of his mouth, and he looked off into space as if remembering something.

"No."

"Well," I squared my shoulders as if announcing that he could shoot me or something. "I'm ready."

It was over in about an hour. Paul had been most gentle and patient, but I had been terrified.

What happened during that hour? Something important and unknown. The story ended with me telling him I wanted to become his wife.

I do, Paul, I could hear myself say. I do.

But first, I would hear him sing.

June 18, Paul turned twenty-three.

June 20 in the Year of our Beatles, 1965 — the best day of my life.

I WOKE EARLY, set my hair and put on my best dress, the baby blue shift with the teardrop cutout at the front that would have shown off my cleavage if I'd had any. The rest of the family were driving to the country for the entire day, much nagging, be careful, don't be late, blah blah blah. I could hardly see, let alone hear.

The matinee was at 3 so I got to the Palais des Sports at 2. Maybe we'd see them arrive, I thought, but no such luck. At 2.30 they let us in. I bought the big souvenir program and turned it to the picture of Paul; I was ready. The Palais was round and gigantic — 4500 seats! — and at 2.30 it was almost empty. In half an hour it was entirely full. Strange — for some reason the audience, all around me, was mostly boys — a wall of boys. Normally, I'd have been interested in my neighbours. But now, my attention was entirely on the stage.

We all clapped our hands, "*Un, deux … un, deux, trois … un, deux, trois, quatre,* let's go!" I wasn't as close to the stage as I'd have liked, but still, the eighth row centre was not bad. A loudspeaker warned us not to use the flashes on our cameras or they would be taken away, and to stay in our seats — any trouble-makers would be removed. Welcome to friendly France, Beatles.

Finally it started.

The first hour and a half were some lousy groups, lots of noise and some booing, including mine. The best known were the Yardbirds. I'd heard of them, but they were awful — just not Beatles. The Beatles' blue amplifiers were on stage, and at one point they brought on Ringo's drums — lots of clapping — with just a piece of paper stuck over "The BeaTles" part. There were millions of cops — when they all filed in, we applauded, so I didn't expect that there would be any screaming. French kids were so obedient.

An intermission was announced, but I was trembling so much, I didn't budge. Finally everybody was in their seats, stamping and howling. The paper had been removed from the drums, and I was holding the picture of Paul and my Brownie camera with the flash off. The announcer came out and got us ready, then counted down, "*Dix, neuf, huit, sept, six, cinq, quatre, trois, deux, un, zero — Les Beatles!*"

He stepped back, a hand pushed aside the curtain and the screams went up to the roof. Scream, yell, sob, cry, adore — THERE THEY WERE, tall and handsome in sober dark grey suits. They smiled at us all screaming away and calmly put on their guitars. Paul came to the microphone and said something, but the screams were so loud that no one heard it. I was waving my picture of Paul, shaking, screaming, stamping my feet, clapping my hands, trying to take a photo and getting ready to pass out, all at the same time.

We in the audience were not in the dark; they left the lights on quite brightly, so I was sure they could see us.

They opened their gorgeous mouths and sang "Words of Love." We calmed down and were quiet during the song, but when it was over and the four heads went down, up went the yells again. Paul again at the microphone, a big smile, even more handsome and cheerful than I'd ever imagined. And he spoke French, with a Liverpool accent. "*Saloo. Mane-tenn-ante notre prochane chawnsown ... chawnsin ... chinsown ...*" He stopped and SCRATCHED HIS HEAD as he tried to figure out how to say, "Now our next song..." Earsplitting screams — he was so adorable. The audience all shouted, "*Oui, oui,*" so he went on, "*s'appaile ...* She's a Woman."

He leaned forward the way he does, to begin to sing. His teeth gleamed, his eyes twinkled. It was at this point that, as I waved his photo, I was sure, oh yes, ABSOLUTELY SURE, that he looked down and saw the girl in the eighth row centre in the baby blue shift with a teardrop cutout. He saw me waving that big picture of his face in a sea of boys and he grinned at me, right at me, inclining his head a bit. One hundred percent sure. I thought my heart would flip right out of my body, like a fish.

If I had died at that moment, it would have been at the pinnacle of my short life. But I did not.

Meanwhile, George was standing lost in the middle, looking at the floor, while John was planted firmly, his feet wide apart, surveying the audience. They sang "I'm a Loser," "Can't Buy me Love," (oooo!), and "Baby's in Black," during which we all swayed back and forth, stamping, clapping, singing, screaming.

Then Paul announced Ringo, who sang "Wanna Be Your Lover," which was the only time the whole afternoon I glanced at him. He just sat there at the back, bashing away; his hair was too long anyway. John's sideburns were a mess, George's hair was curly at the neck and Paul's was perfect, gleaming, shining. I'd always thought his hair was really dark, but it wasn't that much darker than the others.

Then "A Hard Day's Night," introduced by John who only said, "*Mersy*" but then spoke in English. George sang "Everybody's Trying to be My Baby," which was just about the only time I ever looked at him. Then "Rock 'n' Roll Music," "I Feel Fine," the most popular of all, "Ticket to Ride," and then Paul said, "*Main-ten-ant* — our last song." I screamed, "No, no!" but they heartlessly sang "Long Tall Sally," bowed, did a little dance, took off their instruments and left. We howled, screamed, cried. They came back, bowed once more, then dashed off — I'm sure straight out the back way and into a car.

We all stayed a good ten minutes clapping, stamping and yelling, but they didn't come back. I'd done my best — at the end I stood up, waving my arms and my camera wildly, screaming, jumping up and down, calling, "Paul, Paul, Paul!" But he didn't look again or just for a brief second at the first few rows on the second curtain call. I was too numb to feel anything ... sticking to my clothes, boiling yet with goose pimples, close to tears, hoarse, thirsty, lovesick, happy, sad, exhausted. I filed out with everybody and waited, being pushed around by the cops, for half-an-hour by the *sortie*. The *flics* were everywhere, telling us the Beatles had left by the back door, the side door, they weren't going to leave at all. I waited around but saw nothing.

So, in a trance, I went to the metro. There were a lot of *flics* even standing on the platform in the station, and when the packed train passed them, all the kids inside stuck out their tongues and hammered on the windows. I was squashed in near a cute boy who kept talking to me. When he got off, he said, "*Mais vous êtes charmante, mademoiselle.*" I blew him a kiss as my train sped on.

In the blessedly quiet apartment, I had tea and toast with Vache Qui Rit cheese and wrote a note for my father. Until that morning, Dad hadn't known I was going to the second concert in the evening, and when he found out, he was furious, but there was nothing he could do. He had arranged to pick me up at 11, but I wrote to beg him to make it 11.30, drew him a map of where I'd wait, and set off to go back, still numb, clutching my program.

It'd already begun when I got there — the other crummy groups — and again I was sitting in the middle of a group of boys, but these ones were adorable. It made up for the fact that the seat was not only on the side, but on the *wrong side* — John's side of the stage, not Paul's. Why hadn't I figured that out? The boys and I struck up a conversation because I had binoculars and they asked to borrow them. As we talked, I realized to my amazement how well I'd learned to speak this language. The words flowed from me without a pause, and the boys couldn't believe I wasn't French. That's how fluid my tongue was, with shrieking and happiness and lust.

Intermission, the breathless wait — and THEM. Cuter than ever, the audience noisier than ever. It went too fast; I hardly had time to take it all in. Paul was having the time of his life, grinning and smiling. I screamed more than ever. To have them so close and not be able to jump on stage, touch them, talk to them, kiss them — it was excruciating. And Paul didn't look over to the left side once.

They sang and said about the same things, except that they bowed and walked offstage after "Ticket to Ride" and came back for "Long Tall Sally." At the end, the fans surged forward to the barrier, but I couldn't from the balcony. Anyway, Dad was waiting. I didn't want to leave the auditorium, but even more, I didn't want my father to be mad. I rushed out, a few minutes late, and he was there.

As I got into the car, croaking, sweaty, nearly blind, I was dreading his usual sarcastic commentary. But Dad was silent. He just sat, looking at thousands of ecstatic French kids pouring past the car.

"Daddy, it was just the best, the best, I'll never have an experience like that as long as I live, they played all the best songs and they're so beautiful, so handsome and fun and they tried to speak French ..."

As I babbled on the ride home, he didn't make fun or yodel "Yeah yeah yeah." I kept expecting him to, but he didn't. Not once.

FINALLY IN BED at 2.30 a.m., just before turning out the light, I managed a few words in my diary.

June 20

I've seen them. I've seen Them. All of them. All the living, loving, handsome, hairy bunch of Beatles. In real life.
With thousands of others, I've screamed to them. Clapped my hands, walked on air, adored from afar. What a glorious day in the History of Beth.
Oh my Paul, my Beatles — thank you, thank you for

this marvellous night when my life is shining and my
throat hoarse and my memories will stay forever. Thank
you for being you, natural, gorgeous, funny... I love you.
Good night.

And thank you to my father, who, for once in his life, had shut up.

I couldn't sleep, my throat hurt, my heart hurt, I tossed for hours, hearing the songs, watching my smiling Paul, all four of them, over and over.

The papers the next day wrote that at midnight, there had been a fight that overturned a thousand seats. I was sorry to have missed it. Much worse, I learned that bitchy old Jane Asher was there at the same time as Paul, and maybe not even the other Beatles knew. She was not letting him out of her sight! For a moment, I felt such hurt that it almost wrecked the joy of my memories. But only for a moment. Paul would figure out who she was, for sure, and move on.

The articles said how thrilled the Beatles themselves were with the two sold out concerts, because the last time they'd played in Paris, the French didn't like them much. So this day was special for them too.

It was a week before my throat healed and my voice returned to normal. My heart never did. I wondered if anything, ever in my life, would be as spectacular as that day. Impossible.

JUNE 24, FOUR days after the concert, was not the best day of my life.

I was invited to a real French party being given by sixteen-year-old Claude-François, the son of friends of my parents. After we'd met at a dinner with our folks, he asked me to go to a classical concert with him, but I didn't want to go. He wasn't cute or anything, too short and babyish but nice as a friend, so I was glad to be invited to his party and got dressed up — I did my hair, put on my blue dress again, carried my white clutch purse with the golden chain. He lived not in a house, as people did in Halifax, but like everyone else in Paris, in an apartment with high ceilings and decrepit furniture. When I got there, there were already a dozen kids, boys and girls mixing as if this happened all the time, which it did not. Pop music was booming from the record player — Johnny Hallyday, Françoise Hardy, British groups, including mine.

Most of the crowd was older, sixteen at least, the girls, as always, so pulled together and chic, I could never figure out how they did it. Little scarves, sleek hair, the colour and cut of their clothes always just so — even if they weren't beautiful, even if they were actually plain, they looked self-confident and sexy. I always felt awkward and unstylish. But seeing the Beatles had made me feel more mature, and also, at school, I'd realized that I knew how to make people laugh, even French people.

Claude-François introduced me to his friends as *mon amie americaine*, and I sat in the living room, watching kids dance. There was one boy in particular, tall and slender, wearing a brown corduroy suit and a pale blue shirt. Imagine — a suit, how sophisticated. He looked as old as seventeen, his floppy hair not quite long enough, of course, but not bad. He danced easily and was relaxed and friendly with the girls. I watched him out of the corner of my eye.

He was right there, looking at me. "*Vous voulez danser?*" he asked. I couldn't believe it — the boy I had noticed among all the boys had noticed me among all the girls. And luckily, the song that came on was Chubby Checker, so we could twist. I couldn't jive, but I could twist like crazy. While we twisted, we talked. I told him I was really from Canada but pretending to be

American because it was more interesting; that made him laugh. He was from Paris but thought he'd like to go to Canada one day. Yes, come to Canada, Mr. Nice Frenchman, I thought.

There was another fast dance, and he didn't go off to find another girl, he stayed beside me. My face got hot. He was mature. He was smooth and nice and good-looking. The only thing wrong with him was that he wasn't Paul McCartney. We danced the fast dance, and it was wild. I told him about my year at the lycée, about French kids being standoffish, and he nodded as if he knew what I meant.

And then a slow song came on, and he put his arms around my waist and I put my arms around his shoulders and we started to do a slow dance as if we'd been together for a long time. It was romantic, perfect, just as I'd dreamed and dreamed. Our bodies were moving together; I could feel the length of him against me, his arms tight around my waist. He had a spicy smell. I wished I'd worn some of my mother's Chanel. He kissed me softly on the neck; it tickled and almost made me laugh, but there was too much else going on.

And then he bent down, his face came down toward mine, closer, closer, I could hardly breathe, this was happening so fast, I couldn't hear anything except the blood rushing around my body. His eyes were closed, his lips were a little bit open, and then they were pressed against my lips. Everything stopped.

I was at a mixed party in Paris, kissing an older French boy in a brown corduroy suit.

His mouth moved, his lips opened, and something wet and hard pushed against my mouth. Oh my God, his tongue was out and … he was trying to put his tongue into my mouth. This was France; this was a French kiss, I'd heard about them and thought they sounded awful. And this was awful, the hard wet tongue pressing against my lips, trying to push inside. I did not want his tongue in my mouth. I did not want his arms around me. I did not want to be anywhere near him.

I broke out of our embrace, gasped, "*J'ai soif*," and rushed into the kitchen, rubbing away the damp around my mouth. I stood for a moment, regaining my breath. And then I grabbed a glass of Coca-Cola and some food from the table and sat as far out of sight as possible, on top of a metal stepladder tucked in beside the fridge, eating cheese.

Five minutes later, he came in. I didn't want to look at him. What was his name? I'd kissed someone whose name I didn't even know, what a hussy! He stood nearby, puzzled, I could tell. Maybe I'd hurt his feelings. The poor guy probably didn't know that I was fourteen and had never kissed anyone before. I thanked Claude-François and his mother, who was hiding in her bedroom, and left, feeling stupid and immature, but also relieved.

As soon as I got home, I wrote gleeful letters to Hillary and Lea, telling them about my first kiss. I was honest about it being a bit disgusting, but mostly — he was seventeen. He was French. He wore a suit.

In truth, I felt ill when I thought about the whole ridiculous flop.

THAT NIGHT, AS I tossed in bed, a memory came back, something that happened when we lived in the farmhouse in Mill Hill, when I was seven.

I was playing by myself in the farmyard one afternoon, as I usually was, when Simon came by. "Elizabeth, I'm going to visit Rollo," he said. "Want to come?"

My father was back in Halifax, my mother frantic with her courses. Our kind landlords, the Fishers, lived downstairs and had an adopted son called Simon who was not like them. Mum said something about Simon being born a bit wrong. At ten, he was big for his age. Rollo, a school friend of his, lived around the corner with lots of brothers and sisters in a white house. He'd always had a smile for me, and his name was the same as my favourite chocolates.

"Rollo has a television," said Simon. "We're going to watch *Sooty*."

My favourite, Sooty the little yellow bear. "Okay," I said, and walked beside Simon out our gate, down the lane, up the long path to Rollo's. Rollo answered our knock, and we went in. It was white inside too, and quiet and empty. No one else was there. Simon pushed the door closed behind us.

"Well hello, Elizabeth," said Rollo. "Simon was hoping you'd come."

"He told me we'd watch *Sooty*," I said, feeling shy. "Can we?"

"*Sooty*!" He laughed. "Of course we'll watch *Sooty*."

"We'll just make friends first, all right?" Simon said.

"Friends," I repeated.

"We'd like to play a game with you first," said Simon with a smile stretching his face.

"A game?"

"Yes, a funny game." Simon looked at Rollo, who looked away. "This is a jolly game that we'll all play together, only we need to keep it secret from the grown-ups, all right, Elizabeth?"

"I don't know," I said.

"You'll have a lovely time," said Simon, who was moving closer to me. "And then I promise, we'll watch *Sooty*."

A voice was speaking inside me that I had never heard before. It was saying, "Run away." I didn't want to be rude; Rollo had said we'd watch *Sooty*. Perhaps Simon had a funny game in mind, and I'd be sorry to miss it. But I did not want to find out what it was. "Right now," said the voice. My heart hammered.

"I'm sorry, I guess I have to go now," I said, turning and walking fast to the door. I pulled it open and ran down the path home.

I didn't tell anyone what happened. Anyway, nothing happened, and there was no one around to tell.

THE FRENCH BOY in the brown corduroy suit was not like Simon. But the two got mixed up in my mind.

14

July

At the end of the school year, I was walking in my favou-rite part of Paris, near the Boulevard St.-Michel in the Latin Quarter, when I heard a noise, shouting, growing louder. It was frightening — the howling of a mob. Hundreds of students, screeching, chanting, appeared on the other side of the square. What were they going on about? Impossible to tell; they carried no placards and didn't seem to have a direction in mind; they were just making a lot of noise. I huddled in a doorway.

Another sound, like a large motor, and a huge tank-like machine rolled into the square. What was a tank doing here? I wondered. Suddenly, the armoured beast unleashed a blast of water right at the kids. They were struggling to stay upright, knocked down, awash, turning over to hide their faces from the powerful spray. The attack continued until the group dispersed, some still lying on the ground, others running, sodden, dripping.

The tank swivelled and with a grinding of wheels, drove away. The last of the youths got up and squelched off. All that remained was a lot of water and, floating in pools, a scattering of scarves and notebooks.

I pried myself out of the doorway and went home, shaken to see a police force attack its own young people, who may have been a large, noisy group but otherwise were doing nothing wrong. But when I told my school friends about it the next day, they laughed.

"That was only the *monôme*!" Jocelyne cried. "It happens every year when the kids finish their Baccalauréat exams. They have to let off steam, so they do, and then they get wet."

I couldn't believe it. Every year kids let off steam until a water cannon blasted them into submission? What kind of ridiculous set-up was that? One day for sure, I thought, French kids would get sick of being treated like this, and the whole stupid system would blow sky high.

Although I couldn't see any revolution, ever, changing Fortress Claude Monet and Rosy of the Granite Jaw, there were a few things about my school that I'd come to like. In literature class we'd memorized not just the dates of writers, but bits of their plays or poems. We studied six pages of *Phèdre* by Racine for months; impossible to understand, just too complicated, all those dense rhyming couplets. But I fell in love with the poem *"Ma Bohème"* by Arthur Rimbaud and often recited it to myself:

> *Je m'en allais, les poings dans mes poches crevées*
> *Mon paletot aussi devenait idéal;*
> *J'allais sous le ciel, Muse! Et j'étais ton féal;*
> *Oh! La la! que d'amours splendides j'ai revées!*

I could see that dreamy poet, wandering beneath the sky with his overcoat so worn it was nearly transparent, fists in his pockets full of holes, dreaming his splendid dreams of love.

Inspired, I tried writing some poems — one about homework, and a sad one about a boyfriend who left me with only my books for company. But Arthur Rimbaud I was not.

On my last monthly report, I got 18 out of 20 *mauvaises notes*, largely because I'd decorated my *blouse* with writing; even though they were in French, the quotations and scribbles of poetry all over the front and sleeves were not appreciated by Rosy. Still, at the end of the year, I won a prize — for English. Poor Véronique, *petite* egghead Mushroom Girl — this was one class where, even if she'd memorized the entire textbook, which she probably had, she didn't stand a chance. I also came second in history and fifth in French composition, which was a surprise, and thirty-eighth out of thirty-nine in French dictation, which wasn't. My report card was pretty good in everything except *dictée* and *travaux manuels* — basket weaving, ugh! — where I got *médiocre* in the second term and *passable* for the third. And for gym — *beaucoup de possibilités*. Ha ha.

My classmates wanted to make sure that before I vanished, they knew some American slang, so I wrote out a list that they dutifully copied. I half expected them to get out their little rulers and underline this important lesson in red, green and blue.

creep — noun; creepy — adjective
fink
grouch
to dig – (comprendre)
square
flicks — (les films)
shit — très sale!
blue — (triste)
mad — (fâchée)

a drag
hell

and finally

prison — (ecole)

A final cheery chorus of *Phoque*! and I pushed through those heavy doors, leaving Napoleon's rules behind for the last time. It was over. I spoke French, and I had seen the Beatles. Time to go home.

But no. Another joyous surprise, my parents' last great treat — an entire month in the orange tent with my dear family, visiting just about every country in Europe. Nothing to do but grit my teeth and get in the car. We closed up the Gentilly flat, made sure the precious *moquette de tapis* was in its place and drove away. I said a sad *au revoir* to that fantastic city with its zillion things to do — concerts, galleries, museums, theatre, movies — not that they all interested me, but at least, unlike Halifax, they were there. I didn't want to leave Paris; I wanted to transplant my house, friends, school and dog over to France. Maybe I'd come back when I was twenty-one, after university. Soon.

If someone had suggested when we left Halifax that I might ever want to return to Paris, I'd have laughed myself silly.

NO SURPRISE — BEING in the car for hours a day was torture, trying to shut out the scene in front. Dad drove like a Frenchman, fast, impatient, an inch from the bumper of the car ahead. Mum had been in a terrible car accident in Germany after the war and was petrified of driving fast. In sixteen years of marriage, I thought, shouldn't they have worked out some kind of compromise? No, every time we got in the car, Dad drove fast, and Mum squealed, "Gord! Slow down! Agh! You nearly hit him!"

She was writhing and moaning, jamming her foot on the invisible brake, while he zoomed along, pretending she wasn't there.

I will never marry, I thought, blocking the spectacle by getting out my notebook. Why subject yourself to something like that? Two nutcases stuck together forever.

And I wrote a story about travelling with my fiancé, Paul. My most secret story yet, because there was sex in it, sort of — more than in the last one. For four years, my boyfriend Paul and I had spent our holidays travelling all over Europe in his Aston-Martin, without sharing a bed or even a room. Well, I had some principles! We may have been engaged, but we were not yet married.

At last, one night at a hotel in Wales, Paul asked defiantly for one room ... and one bed. I pretended to be outraged, but in my heart, I was overjoyed. Nervous but overjoyed. And things progressed.

> ... Wearing my best nightgown, that for four years I had brought along in anticipation of this night, I got into the left side of the bed, way in the corner, and closed my eyes while he undressed. I could hear him rustling, and the clink of coins as his pants hit the floor. Finally, pajama'd, he got in the other side and turned out the light. I listened to his breathing and could tell that he was nervous ...
>
> Suddenly I yearned to be held in his arms, to feel his warmth next to me.
>
> "Oh, Paul," I groaned, and stretched out my arms to him. He pushed himself over and my desire was fulfilled. He held me tight, tight, and at first I was so happy, I didn't even notice the tears running down my cheeks.
>
> "For four years, we have waited for tonight," I sobbed.
>
> He said nothing, only pressed me tighter until I thought

that he wanted to make me part of him, so that we would never seperate again.

That was the happiest night I have ever passed. After a few hours of bliss, we slept, a sublime sleep of the best dreams. When I woke the next morning, Paul was still sleeping, a sweet and untroubled sleep. I watched him, and knew that we had won each other — and that in a few weeks, maybe all our nights could be like this — legitamately!

I lay down again, joyously reviewing this night, when I felt a hand lightly

Had to stop. I'd finish the story when I knew a bit more.

IN A SMALL town in the south of France, I bought the new *Mademoiselle Age Tendre* with "*Les 4 amours des Beatles*" on the cover, opened the magazine — and burst into tears. There was a devastating picture of Paul with that vampire standing behind him, her claws on his shoulders. She was described, it gave me pain to translate, as "a pretty young girl, blonde, nineteen years old, very long hair which she braids often, joyful hazel eyes."

And then Paul said:

I love Jane, that's certain. Every day I receive anguishing menace letters. "Don't marry, Paul, or we'll kill you." Well I hope I make a cute corpse, because I intend to marry Jane.

MARRY JANE! As soon as possible, he said. "Even within the year"! Marry that self-centred money-grubber! For the first time since my passion erupted, I had real doubts about Paul. Was he that shallow? And anyway, if he loved her so much, I was too honourable to claim him. Jane Asher had won. *Fini with Paul*, I wrote, tears streaming. *Kaput*.

If Paul and I were over, John and I were just beginning. Not a love affair, of course, because of Cynthia — just mutual respect. In the magazine, there was a gorgeous picture of him playing with his little son Julian. Now here was someone I could really love — a good, kind father. And a writer; his new book, *A Spaniard in the Works*, was out, and I couldn't wait to buy it. I'd memorized whole chunks of his first, the hard-to-understand, witty *In His Own Write*.

Luckily, as we drove east through France, there was lots of lovely scenery to look at, not to mention picturesque villages, chateaux, palaces and churches to take my mind off the pain of my breakup. At one campsite, a girl my age in the next tent kept looking at us, feeling envy, I was sure, at this gay and loving family.

If only she knew! Mum was always moaning and suffering from one malady or another. Plus she told me she was having a life crisis and couldn't stand Dad any longer. We had talked seriously several times about divorce or separation, but we couldn't decide on anything. Should she leave him? What would she do? How would she support herself and us? No, it was unthinkable. What would Dad do without her? Would he marry Jadwiga? I could not stop worrying.

Dad and I openly despised each other, and he still delighted in insulting me and contradicting everything I said. But there was one important change — he didn't whack me any more. And I was torn about Dave — he had a good heart, but he was filled with Dad's propaganda.

So I relished those moments when we all laughed together. If only, I thought, they happened more than once a month. Okay, exaggeration. Twice.

DAD HAD ARRANGED to borrow a country house owned by friends in a little town called Sainte-Agnès, way in the mountains above Nice. And then he sprang a surprise, a good one for once — the son of English scientist friends was coming to stay with us. His parents had a conference in Nice and were sparing their son a tedious week with them. Instead he'd have an enthralling week listening to my mother and father fight and watching me and Dave punch each other in the back seat of the car.

Unbelievably, Jonathan was cute. Seventeen, longish dark blond hair, a great smile and that adorable English accent. Wow, I thought, my eyes popping out, what do we have here? My dad had actually produced someone decent.

For once, I was feeling pretty good. Mum and I had been allowed to shop on the Riviera, and I'd bought my first real teenage clothing — low-cut, tight, hip-hugger slacks that made me aware of moving my bum and holding in my stomach, and a tight, pale blue T-shirt that stuck to my body, outlining my curves, such as they were. I was growing my hair and had a new, pinker lipstick. Mum may not have taught me the secret of come hither, but I was, I hoped, figuring it out on my own.

My target was Jonathan. I wore my new outfit to greet him — tried to be both outgoing and shy, to waggle my hips when I walked and look at him sideways from under my hair, as I'd noticed girls doing. It was my goal to appear charming, funny and interested in what he had to say. What he had to say unfortunately was a drag — he wanted to talk about the cello. Of all the instruments, he had to play that one, hence many tedious discussions with my mother about bows and fingering. But I ignored that and tried to be myself only better — a more fun, more self-confident me. *Insouciante*, as the French say, carefree. A complete sham, but I guess he couldn't tell.

By the second day, it was working. He wanted to sit next to

me at lunch and asked me to go to the swimming pool and for walks. It was exciting. And then it wasn't. The boy was desperate to get me alone, and I was desperate to stay right where there were lots of people. The only way I knew to push him back was to be mean, teasing him.

"Jonathan, you're so square with your endless cello!" I said scornfully. And he replied, right in front of my parents, "If you don't stop talking like that, I'll kiss you!" Ugh. My dad laughed, enjoying the spectacle.

Jonathan reminded me of a boy in Halifax. Mark went to another school but lived nearby, and I was pretty sure he liked me. He'd hang around or call because just by accident, he had an extra ticket to something. One day he came over, and I went to the back door to talk to him, forgetting I'd just put a big dollop of Clearasil on a pimple on the side of my face. As we talked, I remembered the pimple and so, for the entire conversation, I had to lean casually against the doorframe with my hand on my cheek.

But Mark was the kind of guy that it didn't matter if he saw a big splotch of Clearasil on your pimple. He just wasn't attractive. At least, he was good-looking and nice, attractive to someone, but not to me. Why was it, I wondered, that girls didn't like boys who were interested in them, only the ones who weren't? How could you help hurting someone when that happened? I didn't know with Mark, and I still didn't know with Jonathan.

By the end of the week, I had to hide in my room from our guest with the hurt puppy eyes. This was a valuable lesson: when you used the come hither look, sometimes they actually came hither, and then you had to figure out what to do with them. Jonathan was ready for something more than flirting. I had tested my hip-huggers, and they worked. That was as far as I was willing to go.

When his folks came to pick him up, he wouldn't even look at me. Mum as usual wanted to discuss it. "What exactly happened with Jonathan, dear? You could have had fun. Such a lovely boy." I just said it was boring, hearing them go on about the bloody cello. That shut her up.

As we drove away, I read my book version of *A Hard Day's Night*, trying to smooth things over with Paul. I didn't want to become a chronic man-hater. Frigid.

IN ITALY, MY new white two-piece bathing suit did the trick. We were camping near Arezzo, and as I was sunbathing on the beach, an Italian boy came over. Giorgio was wearing a skimpy bathing suit that showed too much bulging, but he was very

Us in Pisa.

nice above, with shiny smooth chest and arms. He spoke a little English, so as he sat beside me on the sand, we tried to talk, and later he came to the campsite to find us. He talked to my parents with his bits of English, but he kept smiling at me.

I couldn't believe what was going on. My dad was tickled. "Well, well, an Italian conquest for our little Bethie," he said. "Signora Giorgio," he called me, "the vamp." But I wasn't doing anything this time, not like with Jonathan. Giorgio just appeared.

Nothing serious happened because we were moving on the next day, but he and I did have a sweet goodbye, and he held my hand for a minute or two. My first hand holding, with a complete stranger on an Italian beach. I felt like a complete hussy.

It felt good.

WE READ IN an English newspaper that the government of Canada had authorized a new Canadian flag, not with the Union Jack any more, but two thick red bands with a big red maple leaf in the middle. I drew a version of the new flag — a bit lopsided, maple leaves are not easy to draw — and we stuck it on the back of the Peugeot. At the campsite that night, a red-haired woman walked up — Willa Inglis from Digby, Nova Scotia. She had married the police chief of Bologna and lived full time in Italy. But when she saw our flag, she'd come to say hello and to tell us that though she loved Italy, she really missed home. Me too, Willa. Me too.

AS WE DROVE to Ravenna, I wrote another story about driving in Paul's car. It began with a sublime image of myself as his wife:

> "I love him, I love him, I love him," my heart sang as I washed the dishes, polished the floor and made the beds.
>
> "He is the sweetest man on earth," I repeated as I folded his clothes, washed his socks and tidied his papers.
>
> Work goes fast that way, when one's whole person is singing with love.

Singing with love. That I could do.

But this one had no sex and a very sad ending. Paul was in a hurry to get to John's and drove the Aston-Martin too fast — he would have slowed down right away if I'd asked, but I didn't. He swerved to avoid two little girls crossing the road, and the car crashed.

I was left with my husband, my love and joy, dead in my arms, and two children, crying, by the side of the road.

No no no! I felt guilty for imagining such a terrible thing. And yet I loved that heart-rending scene. And the fact that the next day, after this tragedy, Paul was ready for his next adventure with me.

IN FLORENCE'S GIANT art museum the Uffizi, as we gazed at famous naked Venus on her shell, a tour guide called his group over, pointed to us and said, "Here eesa the kind of beauty who eenspired la maestro Botticelli. Here eesa a reala Botticelli woman!"

He gestured to my mother, and they all swivelled to stare at her. She turned pink and fluttery and smiling and shy. God! I knew we'd never hear the end of it. The one on the clamshell is my mother.

WE CELEBRATED MY fifteenth birthday in exotic Venice with a gondola ride and the usual books, all of them French. I'd discovered George Sand, a great woman writer with a man's name. Dad kept saying I had George Sand eyes. I think he meant it as a compliment, but that poor woman's face was even longer than mine, and her eyes were doleful. Ugly, but a good writer with some interesting boyfriends, Chopin and so on: not such a bad fate.

But what I really wanted, what I'd dreamed of all year besides the *Beatles '65* album, was a silver ID bracelet like the one Paul had (though Paul's was gold). Dad thought ID bracelets were a silly fad, but finally Mum and I found a cheap silver store with the perfect bracelet for $10. It was heavy on my arm, with my name engraved: B E T H. I would never take it off. At least, until I met the right boy to give it to, along with my heart and soul.

Thinking about the man I'd loved for so long, I forgot about my break-up with Mr. McCartney. *Paul does everything I want him to*, I wrote wistfully in my diary, *which a real man wouldn't. They never do.*

AFTER LEAVING VENICE, we drove north on a twisting mountain road toward Switzerland and Austria. Three handsome young men in a red Alfa Romeo convertible were following close behind, and then, at a wider stretch of road, they passed us. Zooming by, they waved and smiled, and we waved back. They slowed, and as we watched, puzzled, the one beside the driver leaned over the side of the little red car, ripping wildflowers from the side of the road. They began to drive so slowly that my father had no choice but to pass them. We all waved again.

And then they revved up and roared by us once more. As they pulled up alongside the Peugeot, the young man on our side stood up. With a wide smile, he pushed the flowers through the open back window of our car, into my hands.

WE SAW MAGNIFICENT things on our trip — Michelangelo's David, the mosaics of Ravenna, Mozart's pad in Salzburg. I appreciated the beauty before me and felt privileged, glad to be there. But the most wondrous sight of my summer was a brown arm covered in dust, holding a tangled bouquet.

DAD SAID HE had one last surprise. "Guess where our boat to Montreal is sailing from, Pupik?" he asked. Nothing could have interested me less. I was lying on the floor of my grandparents' living room in London, waiting for *Top of the Pops* to burst onto their television set. "The most beautiful city on earth," he continued. Oh great — we were going to Prague or some god-forsaken ...

"Liverpool," he said. I shrieked, leapt up and flung my arms around his neck.

WE'D BEEN TO the most beautiful cities in the world, Paris, Florence, Venice — and the place I was most anxious to visit was Liverpool. Which looked, when we arrived, like a large version of Halifax, with its grimy buildings and fishy drizzle. As we only had one day there before getting on the boat for Canada, I was desperate not to waste time in my Beatle hunt. Where to begin? The hotel manager provided a phone book. Remembering that Paul's father's name was James, I wrote down the most important phone numbers and addresses:

> *McCartney J., 106 Delamore St. AINtree 4603*
> *McCartney J., 35 Gloucester Rd., ANfield 6063*
> *McCartney JH. 18 Elm Rd., Woodhey, ROCkferry 4507*

But then I realized: Now what? Phone them all and say, "Excuse me, Mr. J. McCartney, sir, are you Paul's father?" That would be rude. And anyway, what would he say?

"Why yes, little Beatlemaniac, I'm Paul's dad, and I'd just love you to come right on over and scream at me."

I wondered if I should telephone the Liverpool Tourist Bureau to find out where the Beatles lived now. Surely they'd have that kind of information.

Dad announced that he and Dave would go out to a restaurant and a movie, leaving Mum and me free to wander. It wasn't the ideal scenario, exploring the wonders of Liverpool with my MOTHER, but to be honest, I was glad she was there; I wouldn't have had much courage on my own. Anyway, she was eager to come, and she had the purse full of pounds. We hailed a cab.

"To the Cavern, please," I said. O wondrous words.

"I don't mean to be impertinent, luv," the cabbie chuckled in that luscious singsong accent, turning around to look at Mum, "but aren't you a bit above the age range?"

We laughed.

"Wool, you won't have any trubble down there, anyroad," he said to Mum. "But you might," to me, looking at my shoulder-length hair. "They won't know if you're a girl or a boy."

He actually, we learned, had a friend who once dated a cousin of Ringo's wife!

"Tha's it." He pointed down a dark, dirty side road to a scruffy entrance.

We almost lost courage but entered and went down, down, down the steep dank stairs of the Beatle shrine. The whole building was shaking with music. After paying three shillings and signing a book, we entered a noisy, cheerful room divided into three arches — in the middle, chairs and a stage covered with drums and guitars, where a group was to play. I'd seen pictures of those arches, the Beatles as very young teddy boys sweating in black leather playing on the stage beneath them, with Pete Best drumming in those days. I'd figured out from my reading that they had played here for the last time, with Pete's replacement Ringo, exactly two years before, in August 1963. In twenty-four months, my boys had soared from this grubby underground dive to become the most famous band on earth.

The music for the moment was blasting from a record player. Under the outside arches, a few groups talked in huddles; little cliques of boys watched the girls doing syncopated jerky dances to the very loud music. I was surprised; they were decently dressed and well-behaved teenagers — dark suits, slick skirts, very Mod.

"I was expecting a den of iniquity!" I shouted to my mother.

"Can't hear you, music's too loud!" she shouted back, with her hands over her ears. Definitely not cool, but I forgave her. She was forty-one, after all. She must have read my mind, because she said, "Good thing the lights are low; I'm at least double the average age." At least! Though I was feeling out of things and wanted to join one of the clans, male or female, I also thought how *sympa* my mother was, enjoying this as much as I.

Finally the group started, and they weren't bad. As Mum said later, "They were a good group — it was the noise I couldn't stand." I didn't mind, but she did, so we left after a Coke, some sandwiches and fifteen minutes of Liverpudlian music. It was so fab. All Halifax had for teens was the shopping centre and the bowling alley. Miniature golf. Sock hops. This was a CLUB, just for teens.

We wandered around while I bought postcards and John's new book, plus another copy of *In His Own Write*. I already owned a copy, of course, with its foreword by my Paul, but I wanted a copy from Liverpool. Everywhere we went, I thought, "Maybe John stood here." "Maybe Paul pushed through this very door." Every single person sounded like a Beatle. The place was crawling with Beatle. I still wanted to find where Paul was born but gave up, Beatled out. We returned to meet the men and went with them to see *Mary Poppins*.

Mary Poppins! I was angry with myself for being such a

baby and a bad Beatlemaniac. I was fifteen now, old enough to explore these hallowed streets on my own. But I just hung around with my family.

Well, sooomtimes tha' weren't so bad, luv.

FACTS LEARNED IN LIVERPOOL

a. *Cynthia often came to the Cavern to watch John.*

b. *Paul has built a house for himself and his father on the other side of the river, at Badminton*

c. *It used to cost sixpence to get in to see the Beatles, who sang for 2 or 3 hours — night and lunchtime*

d. *They seemed fairly well off and made maybe thirty pounds a week*

e. *John was the scruffiest and had "water marks" — showing where he had washed his face and left the rest*

f. *Maureen and Cynthia — Liverpool*

g. *Patti and Jane — London*

h. *They hardly ever come to Liverpool any more*

i. *The Cavern is on South Matthew St.*

j. *When they first came on, they were thought to be German — "a new group from Hamburg"*

k. *They were a lot wilder in the old days and jumped around, except Pete Best who was very quiet and characterless*

l. *George has built his parents a beautiful white house almost out of town, on a hill, with a big veranda, lots of glass, French doors — "like a castle in clouds." So has Ringo. John?*

m. *Ringo's come back from America because Maureen's baby is due — marriage in April, baby in August (5 months!) She's in Liverpool, I think.*

Anyroad, I was there, the real place where history started and all. It's true, I was only there with my family. But I was there.

ON THE *SS Corinthian*, which wasn't nearly as nice as the *SS France*, I could hardly keep my anticipation under control. Soon the new me would be home — not much prettier, maybe, but much more experienced and sophisticated. In the green diary, the notation for my height now read ~~5' 5". 5' 6 1/2".~~ 5' 7".

I'd been kissed. I'd held hands on an Italian beach. Paul had nodded at me in the eighth row centre. I had hips.

I tried to keep myself calm by reading John Steinbeck's *Travels with Charley*, and of course by writing.

August 25

> *I'm beginning to worry me. I can't become a writer if I don't have an original thought in my head. I feel sickest on reading Steinbeck, my hero at the moment. And even John Lennon, simple Beatle who writes jabberwocky talk, but it's original and funny. Discouraging.*
>
> *Travel betters the wise and worsens the idiot. Which am I? Which have I become?*

One windy afternoon, I wrote a savage new Paul story. Though a few of the others had hinted at sex, this was a different kind that shocked and excited me, even as I wrote. I scribbled quickly, making sure no one could read over my shoulder.

Paul and I were engaged but immoral because we lived together. I often went with him to his work events. One hot summer day the boys were rehearsing when George Harrison, who was crazy about me, lured me to his room. He locked us in and, despite my struggles, tied me up and began to tear off my clothes. Paul heard my cries, broke down the door, knocked George out like in a cowboy movie and ran to free me.

"I was so afraid," he whispered.
I put my head on his shoulder, he picked me up and, the tears still in his eyes, he slowly carried me out.

It all turned out just fine. George apologized to us both, and we became the best of friends again.

Phew.

This one made me tingle — it was so naughty, proof that I had a dirty mind. I would never send it to my friends and had to hide it deep in my suitcase.

Maybe, I thought, maybe it's time to write about something else.

15

September

H OME! Back in my dear little unchanged room, cuddling floppy-eared Brunie who didn't recognize us at first. I ran to get to the telephone before Dave and frantically dialled all my friends. But Hillary was away on vacation, Lea had a summer job, Nancy — something had happened, I learned; she'd disappeared toward the end of school, and no one knew where she was. There were rumours. She didn't leave a note for me.

So my triumphant return wasn't quite so triumphant. I walked around in my blue French hip-huggers, tight French T-shirt and size 85 bra, hoping someone would notice. "Is that you, Beth Kaplan?" they'd say. "Have you ever changed!"

Halifax looked very small now, but its cars looked very, very big. There was peanut butter. Bliss. But no good bread to smear it on. *Everything seems dowdy and inelegant next to Europe. Nature made this country magnificent, and then man made it ugly*, I wrote. *But our house is luxurious and stately next to Gentilly.*

I FOUND THE note I'd hidden for myself. On the envelope: *To Beth Kaplan when she gets back from France.*

June 28, 1964

Dear Beth:

*Well, I guess you're back from France now. Remember me? I'm
the 13 year old Beatlemaniac knowing little French and even
less of France, and hating her father intensely. I wonder what
our apartment will be like etc? You know, of course. I hope
you're a much better person than I am. I'm awful — lazy,
rude, rebellious. You should be mature enough to laugh me
away. I'm young, but old, if you know what I mean.*

    *Well, Beth, now you're almost — or <u>are</u> — 15 and in two
years — university. Now to me, that's a far off dream, but to
you it's just around the corner. Please remember this girl in
your dreams and prayers and know that she's gone forever,
and you're there instead.*

Love

Beth

Age 13

*P.S. I hope you — I — enjoy France. Right now it's just a big
question mark.*

Was I a much better person? No. But I was different. How
could I not be? I visualized my inner self as a house with a bunch
of rooms — one for school, one for friends, family, hobbies,
dreams, books. Now there was a whole room marked "Our
year in Europe," crammed with everything I'd experienced. It was
a very full room.

My mother was different too, more confident, driving the
Peugeot in her snazzy tweed suit, sloshing olive oil and chop-
ping up garlic in our kitchen. Her suppers tasted way better, and
I even enjoyed what she served, occasionally. David had done
really well in his Gentilly school and impressed his Halifax

friends with streams of disgusting swear words in French.

And Dad went back to his lab. I guessed it was hard for him, feeling cheated by his friends and looking for a new job, but he didn't let it show. My parents invited everyone in the physiology department over for dinner, including Don Schmidt, and for the first time they all came. From my room, my little cave of Beatles, I could hear Dad as he told joke after joke, most of them dirty. I desperately wanted him not to show off as much, not to be so loud and funny, as if he had to be. As if he needed to entertain and be noticed and approved of.

Because that was me. Biggest mouth. Best sense of humour. Must go.

HILLY AND I rushed to see the new Beatles movie, *Help!* — which, though not as good as *A Hard Day's Night*, was funny and crazy and wonderful with of course great songs. I was jealous of Eleanor Bron, the actress in the movie, who like me and George Sand had a very long chin and big eyes and weird hair. But perhaps I wasn't quite as strange-looking as Eleanor Bron. We spent the whole day at the movie theatre, saw it three times and bought the album.

Lea got me caught up with what was happening in Halifax, which wasn't much, except when she played me a new singer I'd heard of but not really listened to, called Bob Dylan. He was impressive, a real poet like Rimbaud. Though his voice wasn't great, to say the least, his lyrics made me feel mature just to listen to them.

When Lea heard that the Yardbirds had played at the Beatles concert, she screamed. Maybe I should have listened to them, I thought, at least a bit.

MY MOTHER WAS fussing again about Jadwiga. And about herself; she'd have to find us a house in a new city, but in the meantime should she resume her cello lessons and her recorder group? What did I think she should do?

How should I know?

She and I were much closer now, after being stuck together in France. But still, I couldn't understand how she could be nearly forty-two and not have the slightest idea what she wanted to do with her life. I'd known since childhood I wanted to be an actress and a writer.

As she had been all my life, Mum was in the house all day, sewing and baking, drinking tea, taking lessons and arranging wildflowers. When Dad got home from work, he was full of stories about his colleagues, the new people he'd met, what he was working on. She was the kitchen. He was the world.

The last thing I wanted was to be like Mum. I'd be a wife and a mother, and I'd be an actress and a writer. How I'd do all those things was not clear, but there'd be lots of time to figure it out. I might not marry till I was older — twenty-three, or even twenty-four.

And for sure, when I got married, I'd have a maid.

THE BIG NEWS was that, instead of going to grade eleven at QEH, the big public high school, I'd be going to the Halifax Grammar School, the boys' school Dad had founded which, while we were in France, had begun to accept girls. It was just around the corner, and it was really good academically. But the most important thing: on the first day, I walked into the classroom to find fifteen boys and only two other girls. I thought I'd pass out.

Fifteen sixteen-year-old boys! My Paul would be in for some competition.

Within two weeks, my mind and body were exploding, and I had a crush on half my classmates. I hated how I behaved at first, joking loudly, pretending to be cool and loose, boasting about getting kissed in Paris. The other two girls weren't all that pretty either, luckily, but Karen was smart with very big breasts, and Lillian was brilliant and organized and a hard worker.

So I had to be funny.

One of my classmates was Andrew, the nice boy who'd hugged my strapless bra flat at the HLC dance. We started to write notes to each other, especially in French class, where I didn't have to pay any attention at all. I asked him about boys. About sex.

"Boys like girls who give," he scribbled in answer to one of my lists of queries.

"What does 'give' mean?" I wrote back, breathless.

"Hand rub, upper half," was his precise reply.

Hand rub, upper half. That meant boys would like you if they could take off your bra and rub your bare breasts.

I guessed that would be okay with the right boy. Whoever that was.

IN OCTOBER I stopped playing the field and picked the boy, of all fifteen, whom I'd adore. It was the one hundred percent least likely boy in the class for me — Alan. Al was a horny wolf who drove a little red 1964 Buick and had been seen removing Patsy Charles's bathing-suit top with one hand while steering his motorboat around the Arm with the other. He hated school, had never read a book for pleasure in his life and was a right-wing capitalist who liked the Beach Boys and made fun of Bob Dylan. "How does it FEEL?" he'd yowl, making Dylan's poetic "Like a Rolling Stone" sound sexual. Alan made everything sound sexual. That was his special gift.

I had not one iota of respect for him. Every molecule in my body was nuts about him. It was like being insane, like my mind and body belonged to someone else. A boy as unlike Paul as it was possible to be — not gentle and kind, but mocking and harsh — and yet I wanted to be near him so badly, I thought of nothing else most of the day and night.

Though others in the class could see my real feelings, I covered everything up to Alan himself, making fun of him with mocking words. I called him "capitalist pig" or "bourgeois aristocrat," and he called me "crazy socialist." I didn't even know what a socialist was, except that it meant left-wing and compassionate and for the people, not a selfish fat cat like Al with his Buick and shiny loafers and slicked-back hair, all of which I hated. We argued about the Vietnam War — "America out!" "Save the world from Communism!" — except I still knew nothing about the Vietnam War, and neither did he. We argued about the Canadian election in November, I for the NDP, he for the Progressive Conservatives, and then the Liberals won. A new politician from Quebec, Pierre Trudeau, shocked people by walking into the House of Commons wearing sandals. Al thought that was disrespectful. "Canadian men don't wear sandals," he said.

"Shows how much *you* know," I said. "My dad always wears sandals."

Mind you, my father was not Canadian. It was easy to tell Dad was American — he was too loud to be from Canada. Listening to him rant about some petty thing an official at the university had just done to him, I wondered if he was angry all the time because the country he had to live in was just too mealy-mouthed for him. Dad had taken his first job in Canada because an American politician called Joseph McCarthy was persecuting left-wing people and making it impossible for them to work in the States. If Dad had been able to stay in the country of his birth, where there were lots of argumentative, forceful people like him, would he have been less frustrated? Would he have been calmer?

Oh well. No point asking.

ALAN HAD NO idea that after our nasty fights at school, after pouring insults on his head, I went home to scribble in my diary about how much I desired him. We had a bunch of spare periods together, the best part of school. One day in spare, he actually told me he was discouraged about his love life, and I told him he would never have trouble finding girls.

"Your animal magnetism will always appeal to girls," I said.

"But Beth, does it appeal to you?" he asked, locking my eyes with his, and for the briefest second, I wondered if he really cared — for me.

Of course not.

His hand reached out, and almost tenderly, he disentangled my hair from the collar of my blouse. We sat silent for a few seconds, time that stood still. And then the bell rang.

Why couldn't I be the kind of girl for a boy like Al? Why was I always the wrong girl?

The Student Council, of which Alan was President, held a Slave Day to raise money. All the girls were auctioned off to be slaves to the boys for one day. Lillian went for $1.90, Karen for $2.50, and I — to Al — for $2.85. Even with my inferiority complex, I had to note that my price was the highest. Not the highest in the school — Ellen, a beautiful blonde two grades below, was bought by a consortium for $5.00. I had to carry Al's books all day and help him on and off with his coat. I was wild with happiness.

But the next minute, he'd say something crass, and I loathed him. He was a Neanderthal sex-maniac, and I would never speak to him again. There were lots of other boys. I would shower attention on them.

It was like being two different girls, the one who adored Al, and the one with a brain.

ONE DAY, I heard him tell Andrew that he'd lost his French grammar textbook. My heart skittered; I knew all the grammar.

"Hey moneybags," I said, "you can have my book."

"Thanks, Beth," he said, surprisingly without sarcasm.

My heart bashed against my ribs all day, to think of his hands holding something of mine. After school, as I was packing up my stuff, he came over.

"Want a drive home? Then I can get the book."

A drive. In the Buick. I'd never been in a boy's car before, too bad I only lived around the corner. His car smelled manly, like him — Brut. His hands were smooth, not hairy. His eyes were black. We sat side by side. My body was buzzing so fast, I thought I'd disintegrate.

"Nice street, Kaplan," Al said. "Nice house for a socialist."

Please don't let the house be crazy, I prayed, picturing Mum's recorder group tootling away. But she was in the kitchen, unpacking groceries like a normal person. A new prayer — please don't let her say anything embarrassing. She knew about my big crush, of course. She knew every single thing that happened in my life. Even if I tried to keep something to myself, her blue eyes could pry it out of me, instantly.

Alan J.L. Pritchard was standing in my kitchen.

"Al's come for a book," I said. "Mum, this is Alan."

"Hello, Mrs. Kaplan," he said, polite and handsome, shaking her hand.

Mum said, "Alan. I've heard so much about you."

No! I thought. Don't!

"All of it bad, I'm sure," he said, and they both laughed. I had to get him out of there.

"I'll get the book," I said and ran upstairs, returning puffing to thrust it at him. They were chatting about the early days of the school, Mum gazing intently with her hypnotic eyes. I got him away, outside. He leaned against the car.

"Your mother's beautiful, Kaplan," he said. "What happened to you?"

IN SLOW MOTION, underwater, I registered what he'd said. She was beautiful. I was ugly. No one had said it out loud before.

No, I thought, breaking through to the surface, filling my lungs. No! He was joking, probably, in that hard, mocking tone we both used.

"Just unlucky, I guess," I said. We both looked away. Maybe he knew this time, he'd gone too far.

Maybe he meant what he said. What happened to you?

I didn't watch him drive away.

"He seems nice," said Mum, eager to talk.

"Well he isn't," I said. I went up to my room and put on Paul's "Yesterday" over and over. I wanted to drown in that song. How could a piece of music be so perfect? I loved Al so much, I could hardly breathe. It was not her fault she was alluring. My best friend. My enemy.

Where was my Paul? I opened the story scrapbook and read the first long one, where he helped me with my math homework. It made me laugh and cry. She was so silly then, that girl, innocent and young. Now she was old, a beaten ugly old greyhound that couldn't run any more and that nobody wanted.

That nobody would ever want.

AT THE END of October, the four members of the best band in the solar system were awarded a great honour in England, an MBE. Lots of stuffy people sent their MBE's back in protest, which even

Dad thought was ridiculous. And they released a new album with a strange name. *Rubber Soul* was fab gear, especially because of "Michelle," a romantic ballad where Paul spoke some French. Did he write it in Paris, I wondered, and did he remember the girl in the eighth row centre waving his picture? He sang two songs about unhappy love, "You Won't See Me" and "I'm Looking Through You." Were he and what's her name breaking up? Was there hope?

I felt the weight of the ID bracelet on my wrist.

And the strange "Norwegian Wood," where John slept in a bathtub and then maybe set fire to some girl's furniture. One song — "In My Life" — was one of the few ballads I was crazy about sung by someone other than Paul. Dear old John. So sad and true.

AT SCHOOL, I'D made friends with one of the older boys from the grade above. Jim was twenty, had quit school to work for a while and then come back. I wasn't attracted to him, but he was a good listener. I confided in him how confused I was, especially about sex.

"Maybe if you had some experience," he said, "you wouldn't be so hung up about it."

"But how will I get experience when I don't go out with anyone?"

"Well — how about this? I could give you necking lessons," he said. "I know quite a bit. You could practice on me."

It made sense. It would be good to practice on someone who knew what he was doing. So one December night, when my family was out, he came over. It was a bit awkward at first — we hardly knew each other — but he sat down beside me on the sofa and took off his glasses.

"Ready?" he said, smiling.

"Okay," I said, not smiling. I had brushed my teeth about eight times. He slowly leaned his head in, his eyes closed, and his lips met mine. We sat there with our lips locked together, moving around a bit, for fifteen seconds or so. He smelled nice, and the kiss was minty, probably my Crest. His lips were soft. I worked out how to breathe through my nose and kiss at the same time.

We broke apart. "That was great, Beth," he said. "Now here's Lesson Number One: close your eyes."

I felt like a fool. But we tried it again a few more times, and then, though it looked like he would've been happy to go on, I'd had enough. Necking lessons were okay, but really, I realized, when I was crazy about someone, it would probably be quite a different experience. Maybe this was not so useful after all.

I felt nothing, except glad that I'd learned how to breathe and that he had not tried to do much with his tongue.

"Thank you, Jim, that was very nice," I said at the door, and shook his hand.

Dec. 10 1965

How weird I feel! Suddenly full of strange surges of grief and joy, impatience, of regret, of longing. I haven't felt so strangely since we left France. Longing, again, for something — something richer than logarithms! Something beyond the horizin, out of reach. I feel as if I'm going insane. And I keep reaching for this journal, 'cause I can keep pouring out these emotions to you. Friends or a mother can get tired of my babblings, but paper can't.

I feel calmer already.

As I scribbled, the grooviest new single flowed out of my transistor — "The Sound of Silence," by a group with the queer name

Simon and Garfunkel. Without music, I thought, the earth would grow dark, and we would die.

THE FREEDOM SINGERS were five tall Negro men and one small white guitarist who came to Halifax in December to sing to the local people about racial integration and social justice. Dad was a leader, organizing and fundraising. We had a reception at our house, with much of the Negro community of Halifax crowding into our living room to meet the Freedom Singers, and Dad didn't even flinch when a large lady sat on his prized Danish modern teak coffee table and it broke. Matt, handsome like the boxer Cassius Clay — whose name for some reason was now Mohammed Ali — and stubby Marshall were even billeted with us. I went to their concert at the university, proud that they accepted and maybe even liked me, though I was white. *The greatest thing since the Beatles*, I told my diary.

Best of all, I got to tell Al about the Negroes living in my home, about desegregation and the Student Nonviolent Coordinating Committee. Two of them had even sung at a civil rights protest concert with Bob Dylan and Joan Baez! Al didn't have a clue what I was talking about.

Bill, their guitarist, was earnest and smart, and I developed a huge crush on him. He told me what the others had been through, the horrors of their southern homes. Chico was nearly beaten to death by the police while an FBI officer stood by, making notes. His crime? Carrying food to the hungry, thirsty Negroes waiting in the hot sun to register as voters. And Matthew had a souvenir of the Ku Klux Klan on his head — nineteen stitches. I told Bill I felt horribly privileged and ill-informed.

And then Bill said, "How old are you, anyway?" When I said, "Fifteen," he made a face.

"I thought you were much older than that," he said. Far out!

He was twenty-three, just like Paul. Mature and a good guitarist, dedicated to this important cause. Like Bob Dylan, he was spiritually, not physically, attractive, a small white passionate musician from New York with a big nose, a big guitar and lots of heart. I felt stirrings in my own heart and in the rest of me too. He took me to see the tragic movie *The Pawnbroker*, which triggered so many tears, man, I thought I'd be washed right out of the cinema.

But they were on tour, and they had to move on. Bill's father owned a factory where they sewed on the little hooks and eyes that attached to the back of brassieres. Before leaving, he gave me a sample — a piece of white material with holes where the bra hooks would go. Outside, after I'd taken a picture of them in our driveway with my Brownie camera, Bill blew me a kiss and called, "Dig you, baby." Wow. I stuck the sample in my diary and hoped he'd come back.

In my diary, also — and I did know it was bizarre — well, my body was producing hair in various places, and a stiff little hair started to grow from a mole on the right side of my chin. I borrowed my father's tweezers and yanked the hair out, but I didn't want to just throw it away; it was a historical artefact and part of me. So I stuck it under a piece of scotch tape in my diary. The girls at school were talking about shaving their legs, which sounded painful, I would never do that. But every time I plucked a hair from my mole, I preserved it under the piece of tape. It grew to be quite a collection.

One evening, Dad caught me delving in his shaving kit, and I confessed why I was borrowing his tweezers. What mole? he wanted to know, and inspected it closely.

"Don't mess around with moles," he said. "Don't pull anything out any more." He sounded really concerned. In bed that night, hearing again the worry in his voice, I had a blinding thought. Maybe that means he loves me. Maybe he loves me.

That must mean he loves me.

December 29, 1965

God, we teenagers are marvellous! Poor old bumbly adults, pottering along the beaten path ... They can't imagine the exhilaration of speeding in a car, the sheer joy of doing wild dances, of laughter and pranks, of rebellion and discussions. Please, let me stay young in mind all my life! Beth, please don't betray yourself in your old age by allowing your brain to age and wither, by sitting back and condemning youth, by cutting yourself off ... Live! Be young, vital, gay!

I'm so glad to be happy and free!! I love being a "normal" teenager, wearing bell-bottomed trousers and a sloppy shirt

and no shoes. Loving Al. Loving life. Loving me.
I feel as if I could save mankind single-handed!

And for a while there, I really did.

ON THE LAST night of December, Mum, Dad and I were sitting at the kitchen table eating Mum's delicious turkey soup and homemade brown bread when they started talking about Dave, who was at his best buddy Hughy's. As usual, they were fretting about how restless he was in school, always fooling around. Dad was upset that his son wasn't doing well in the very demanding school that had been created just for him.

"He's lazy and plays the fool," he said. "I've got to knock some sense into him. And those friends of his are idiots."

"They may look like idiots to you, Dad," I said, "but they're his friends."

"I don't care," he replied. "My son should not be consorting with morons instead of tending to schoolwork."

For the first time, I didn't just scram, out of fear. Because he was wrong.

"You know, Dave needs support," I said, aiming at them both, my mother wringing her hands, my father hard and impatient. "School isn't a cinch for him. That's just not the way his brain works, so he shuts off. He needs you to help him figure things out. He needs patience."

What'd gotten into me? I got ready to duck.

"Hmmm," Dad said. "Well. That's what you think?"

"Oh Gord," said Mum, getting out her Kleenex. I felt my shoulders relax a bit and decided, what the hell.

"Daddy," I said, taking a deep breath, "did it ever occur to you that maybe we're not like you? Both me and Dave …"

"Dave and I," he said.

"Dave and I ... might be good at different things than you. He does things his way. And that's okay. He's a nice guy with lots of friends."

He sat looking at me.

"Bethie," he said, "perhaps I'm too hard on him. Is that what you're saying?"

"Yes. That's what I'm saying." And, I wanted to add, you're too hard on me too.

"I'll have to think about that," he said. "I've never had to worry about you; you've always been on the straight-and-narrow. But I do worry about your brother. I have the right to my concerns about him, don't I?"

"Concern is one thing. Jumping on him is another."

"I'm doing my job, as a father."

WE WERE TALKING like grown-ups — a real conversation, back and forth, me and Dad. He had an amazed expression, as if it had just occurred to him that I was a real human being with a brain. While we talked, he took out a Cuban cigar, his usual after-dinner Tueros. Before lighting it, he pulled off the gold paper ring that encircled the cigar, as he'd been doing since I was little, and slid it onto my finger. I waved it around to catch the light.

We talked about people, like him, who are lucky enough to find jobs they enjoy.

"Freud said that human beings need two things, Pupik, love and work," he said, exhaling clouds of stinky smoke. "But there's a third — the need to believe in something bigger than yourself. All human societies have needed that. Some kind of god."

"So what do you believe in that's bigger?" I asked.

"Science," he said, "the great mysteries of biology and genetics. And music. What about you, Bethie?"

He was asking me a question and waiting for a response.

229

"Music — oh yeah. And love."

We smiled at each other. For a second, I felt like someone else. Then he looked at his watch. He'd been offered a job at the University of Ottawa, he told me, and was meeting someone to discuss it.

"You'll be happy to hear," he said as he stood up, "there's a superb restaurant at the Faculty Club that serves *alouettes farcies*. Stuffed larks."

So happy to hear that.

Ottawa. Though it meant leaving behind almost everything I cared about, I wouldn't mind moving there. He enfolded me in a hug. Muffled in my father's scorched smokey smell, I wished I could capture this feeling, so it would never go away. Because I knew it would.

"I'm proud of you," he said.

"And I'm proud of you," I said back.

Why couldn't parents just be one thing, so you knew where you stood? You had to be a genius to figure out how to live with them.

Dad disappeared to get his coat, and there was Mum, beaming. "Come, my love, let's have a cup of tea," she said, rising to plug in the kettle. She wanted to talk about Jadwiga, or the family finances, or to draw from me what was going on with Al and the other boys at school. I didn't know how to say no to her. I loved my mother so much, it felt like a drug I could not live without. Poor Mum was so sensitive and tenderhearted, with so little self-confidence, she could not survive without me to help her see straight.

But this once, I did not want to bare my soul or listen to her bare hers. "Sorry Mummy, later, okay? A big assignment to start," I said. Leaving her was hard but doable, once in a while.

As I creaked up the familiar stairs, I wondered if a talk like the one Dad and I just had would ever happen again. That was the great thing about life — there was always hope. Or, as I could now say with a pleasing rasp in my throat, *il y a toujours de l'espoir.*

HOW I WOULD miss my cozy haven, its windows over the garden and trees, the now-invisible Twenty Wildflowers. But Dad had said he'd need to sell the house. Time to unstick the pictures from the wall and store them in the Beatle scrapbook. I changed into my new blue jeans and closed the bedroom door, so I didn't have to hear Dad yelling at my brother. Putting on *Another Side of Bob Dylan*, which Doug at school had lent me, I got to work.

Dylan's songs were so intense. So *long*.

It was possible, I couldn't help but think, that Doug liked me. He brought me things and was just there a lot, like I was just there for Al. Doug was tall with longish hair and a sporty lean body; though a whiz in school, he was not an egghead. But Doug was soft. Trusting. He was just too vulnerable, too nice for me.

I decided to ask for a guitar for my sixteenth birthday and grow my hair long and straight, like Françoise Hardy, and write poetic protest songs and sing them. I'd be hip. A beatnik.

Dylan was singing that he was so much older then, he felt younger now. I felt like that too.

PAUL, MY LOVE, I said to him, taking down my favourite photo. It's been nearly two whole years since I first heard you sing. You were there whenever I needed you. We've grown up together.

But most of the time now, Paul, I'm dreaming not about you but about Al — Al driving me home again and seizing me in his arms and kissing me in the driveway. Me transforming him from a jerk into a gentle left-wing guy who still sports a sexy arrogant scowl.

No. Impossible. The boy would never change. Even as I dream about Al and me, I told Paul, scotch-taping him into the precious scrapbook, I know it won't happen. I absolutely do not want it to happen. Al sticking his tongue into my ear … Part of me grimaced at the thought. The other part was frantic to make it real.

I unstuck the last picture from the wall and pressed it to my lips. And then into the book.

And I thought, right now Mr. McCartney is carrying me in his heart as I carry him in mine. I was sure of it, busy, brilliant and far away though he was. How could I have felt so much for him for so long, and him not know it? He must know it.

THERE WAS ONLY one way to sort out my lunatic loves and the lunatic world and my amazing lunatic self. The green plastic French journal was filled and falling apart. I took out a fresh, just bought yellow Hilroy scribbler, sat at my desk in front of the black nighttime windows, and opened to page one.

*With apologies to Jane Asher, who by all accounts
is a very nice person with no major alcohol problem.
And to sweet George Harrison also.*

Acknowledgements

HEARTFELT THANKS TO:

— The many wise, patient and skilful friends and colleagues who read, edited and in every way encouraged the slow birth of this memoir, especially Patsy Ludwick, Margaret Davidson, Chris Tyrell, Wayson Choy, Bruce Kellett, Suzette Couture, Elke Town, Sally Keefe-Cohen, Rosemary Shipton, Kate Henderson, Iris Turcott, Debby de Groot, Marilyn Biderman, Barbara Berson and Stella Walker; my Thursday group, especially Chris Cameron and Jason Allen; and the last draft readers, Chris and Cathy, Anne-Marie and Jim, Lani, Paul, Laurel, Lesley, Duncan, Carole, Carol and many others.

— Donald Bastian for his meticulous editing and production, Tannice Goddard for her great design and Alanna Cavanagh for her glorious cover.

— My dear blog readers — I'm glad you are there, whoever and wherever you are.

— My neighbours, especially Monique, Jean-Marc and Richard, Mary and Malcolm, Gretchen and Jack; HGS school-mates Ian, Chris and Ron; Barbara and the Rea family; and

Mr. Fix-It John Greeniaus, without whom I'd go mad.

— My role models at the Y, Judy's meditation group, John Sinclair and Dr. O'Neil. Ditto.

— Friends in Europe, especially all the Blins; family in New York, especially Ted Kaplan; and the Kushners, who have opened the door to Paris for me again.

And ...

— My beautiful and loving mother, who saved every word I ever wrote, making this book possible. You were right, Mum – I do regret quitting the piano.

— My magnificent father, *grace à qui je parle couramment le français, comme lui.* And who gave so much to his adopted country.

— My brother, MGK. What a thrill, not long ago, to enjoy a Paul McCartney concert with you — you, a John Lennon man through and through.

— My children, Anna and Sam, who taught me what true love is.

— My grandson, Eli, who goes on teaching me, every day.

— The Beatles, who have brought and still bring immeasurable joy to the world.

And most of all, to Sir Paul, who for more than fifty years has filled our lives with music. One of my fondest memories, Paul, is of my parents, who became huge Beatle fans, dancing around the kitchen to their favourite song "When I'm Sixty-four."

Sixty-four seemed impossibly old to me back then, as it must have to you when you wrote the song at the age of sixteen.

As I write this, my friend, I'm about to turn sixty-four.

Doing the garden, digging the weeds — who could ask for more?

ABOUT THE AUTHOR

Beth Kaplan's book about her great-grandfather, *Finding the Jewish Shakespeare: The Life and Legacy of Jacob Gordin*, was hailed as "witty, shrewd and elegant" by famed playwright Tony Kushner. For years a professional actress, Beth Kaplan now teaches memoir and personal essay writing at the University of Toronto and Ryerson University; in 2012 she was given U of T's Excellence in Teaching award.

Early readers of *All My Loving* expressed great interest in her fascinating family, which is the story she is writing next.

Follow Beth's blog on her website www.bethkaplan.ca.